Protecting Privacy in Two-Way Electronic Services

by David H. Flaherty

Foreword by Ronald L. Plesser

Mansell Publishing Limited
London

Communications Library

Protecting Privacy in Two-Way Electronic Services

British Library Cataloguing in Publication Data

Flaherty, David H.
  Protecting privacy in two-way electronic
  services.
  1. Telecommunications—Security measures
  I. Title
  621.38′0413′0289   TK5102.5

  ISBN 0-7201-1744-5

Mansell Publishing Limited
(A subsidiary of The H. W. Wilson Company)
6 All Saints Street, London N1 9RL, England

First United Kingdom edition, 1985.

Printed in the United States of America

10   9   8   7   6   5   4   3   2   1

Table of Contents

For Sean

Foreword

Interactive two-way communication poses a unique challenge to the traditional concepts of privacy protection. The coming into existence of two-way services has endowed the local cable or videotex operator with the ability to become the repository for a significant amount of personal information about an individual, ranging from taste in movies to financial transactions, from credit purchases to medical history records.

Until recently consumers have usually dealt directly with companies providing services to them. Through the use of interactive cable a great number of diverse consumer transactions can now be carried out by dealing directly with only one entity—the cable operator.

What is unique is not that individualized data are maintained and disseminated in the course of implementing interactive services, but rather the potential for all this disparate information to become collected and stored in one place. This may lead to the perception that operators of two-way services may create profiles on individuals or, even worse, that they may provide an opportunity for surveillance by law enforcement officials and others. In this book David Flaherty meticulously identifies all the potential activities of interactive services and the current responses to them on the part of the public, industry and government.

More importantly, Professor Flaherty places the challenge where it belongs—with the cable and interactive service industries. Certain companies such as Warner Amex and trade associations such as the Videotex Industry Association have responded to the problem by adopting voluntary subscriber privacy codes. These codes are significant because many of them become part of subscriber contracts and become binding. Therefore, while voluntary in the inception, these codes become enforceable requirements.

The development of these codes is important for two reasons. First, they are an appropriate response to an issue of public importance. Second, they greatly increase public confidence in the use of interactive services. The public may resist using two-way services if it believes, rightly or wrongly, that information gathered as a result of its subscribing to these leaves individuals open to surveillance by industry or government. An affirmative and positive response by the companies themselves will go a long way to dispel this perception.

The rules that companies apply to themselves by restricting their use and dissemination of individualized information will likely become the rules that will govern all interactive services in the future. By voluntarily developing and enforcing their own privacy codes, the industry can in effect write its own rules.

The one area which cannot be controlled by voluntary action is government access to interactive records. An electronic mail company, for example, has recently gone to great lengths to resist U.S. government access to its records. Government prosecutors may continue attempting to obtain private individualized data from cable companies offering interactive services unless a law which regulates government access to those types of records is enacted.

On the federal level in the U.S. legislators have recently added a privacy provision to the cable deregulation bill. This provision, as adopted by the relevant House Committee, creates nationwide standards and limits government access to cable information. Its privacy elements are closely patterned after the Warner Amex Cable Privacy Code issued and adopted in 1981. Industry participants in the U.S. have been first to respond to identifiable concerns; now the government's actions are limited to codifying the standards set by industry.

David Flaherty is an expert on the topic of privacy in the United States and Canada. He brings to the issue the temper of an academic and the instincts of an entrepreneur. His work in the area of cable privacy must be considered the definitive work on the subject.

Ronald L. Plesser

August 1984
Washington, DC

Ronald L. Plesser was a consultant in the preparation of the Warner Amex Code of Privacy. He served as general counsel to the U.S. Privacy Protection Study Commission from 1975 to 1977.

Preface

This book is about challenges to the protection of personal privacy posed by two-way information technology. The discussion is set in the context of the cable television industry and two-way cable technology in particular, although telephone-based interactive services are also discussed. The intended audiences are federal, state, local and provincial governments and regulators, the cable television industry, companies offering two-way services and the general public as current and potential consumers of interactive services. Since each audience starts with a different level of knowledge, I have presented in detail the material that led to my conclusions and recommendations and suggest that readers with specialized background read the book selectively.

This book is a revised and updated version of a report, dated April 30, 1983, to the Policy Planning and Research Division of the Ontario Ministry of Transportation and Communications. The Communications Division of the Ministry determined on its own that the privacy aspects of two-way cable services required examination and then generously funded the research. I am grateful to Dr. Gordon Hemsley and Dr. Martha Fletcher for their guidance and support. The original report has been considerably reworked to reflect a North American perspective and to incorporate additional research on telephone-based interactive services.

I have tried to provide information that is current through July 1, 1984, but new developments in the cable television and telephone industries are constantly occurring. However, the basic privacy issues at stake are independent of the implementation of particular services.

I would like to acknowledge the contributions of a number of people. My colleague at the University of Western Ontario, Neil J. Vidmar, who directed our sample survey of attitudes towards personal privacy in London, Ontario, has been supportive and critical of my work. (The survey was carried out in the context of a study of overall attitudes to modern technologies, such as computers, so as not to bias the results in favor of privacy.) Lewis Auerbach of the Canadian Radio-television and Telecommunications Commission (CRTC) has generously guided me into the mysterious regulatory world of broadcasting in Canada. Terence J. Donohue, at one time a law student at the University of Western Ontario, rendered considerable assistance in locating library materials, as did reference librarians at the University of Western Ontario, the Canadian federal Department of Communications and the CRTC. I have had the benefit of several careful readings of the text by my current research assistant, Peter J. Harte. Frances Kyle, my former secretary, endured the emergence of the report with her customary tolerance and good humor (whatever "moments" she had, she kept them from me); Lizbeth Carruthers and Marnie Cudmore have done similarly fine work on the final volume. I am also grateful to the large number of people associated with the cable television and telephone industries in Canada and the United States who allowed me to interview them for this study. I owe a special debt of gratitude to the following individuals for their contributions: David P. Ballard, Perrin Beatty, Robert Gellman, Michael Hind-Smith, James Hum, B. C. McFarlane, Richard H. McLaren, Ronald L. Plesser, Norma Rollins, Frank Spiller, Alan F. Westin, Robin White and Zavis Zeman. I would also like to thank Knowledge Industry Publications editors Ellen Lazer and Fran Epstein who devoted much time and effort to shaping and structuring my manuscript.

Finally, I want to mention my family, Kathy, Sean, Mike and Bobby, since they always look for their names in print; they also put up with me.

David H. Flaherty

London, Canada
August 1, 1984

1

Introduction

The 1980s are witnessing the introduction of many new forms of information technology, including two-way, or interactive, television services delivered over coaxial cable or telephone lines into individual homes. In contrast to traditional one-way systems, where, for example, television programs are simply delivered to a household, two-way systems also involve the return of information from the household to or through the headend computers of the system operator. With interactive opinion-polling, for instance, viewers can respond to questions about political and social issues by using a keypad attached to a television set. Subscribers to teleshopping services will be able to view pictures and information about products that can then be ordered by using push-button telephones to charge items to their credit cards. Other two-way services that telephone and cable companies have already introduced or have in an advanced state of development include pay-per-view programs, security and medical emergency services, tele-education, telebanking, information retrieval and videotex.

COLLECTION OF PERSONAL INFORMATION

The new services described above will offer many benefits to consumers, but the impact of this technology has a potentially darker side. Interactive services involve the collection of a great deal of detailed information about users, which could, by design or by accident, ultimately challenge their privacy.

As *New York Times* reporter David Burnham noted in his book *The Rise of the Computer State* (1983), interactive systems permit for the first time the collection and linkage of transactional information about the events of daily life inside homes. They can record transactions between a user and a financial institution, purchases made by individuals and families, and television program choices of particular households. For example, if X-rated movies become a staple product of pay cable television, as has occurred in

1

some U.S. cities, monthly billing records of cable companies could yield a listing of subscribers that would be quite different from the *Social Register.*

Furthermore, the use of interactive systems does not necessarily mean that specific responses in all cases have to be initiated by the subscriber. Unlike traditional television systems, where a company disseminates programming without any knowledge of who is watching it, two-way systems make it possible for a cable company to know exactly which subscribers are using which services at any given time. Through a process called channel monitoring, cable operators' headend computers can automatically check every few seconds to see what channel is being watched in a particular household, and this can be done without the viewer's awareness.

COLLATION AND DISSEMINATION OF PERSONAL INFORMATION

The wealth of personal data available to system operators through interactive services could, if controls are not introduced, be collated to produce detailed profiles of the individuals concerned. The storage and possible dissemination of sensitive personal information through the integrated computer operation of affiliated companies could pose a threat to personal privacy.

It is more than likely that if detailed personal information exists it will be used, often in ways and for purposes that were not originally anticipated. If a system such as two-way cable television records personal information in an automatic fashion, the data can be stored, re-used and obtained by third parties, including the government, law enforcement agencies, private investigators, lawyers and providers of marketing services.

In particular, it must be kept in mind that the detailed information about subscribers that can be collected through these services has enormous attractions for marketing purposes. Moreover, the North American cable industry is facing a variety of economic pressures. In order to justify their investments and return a profit, will it become necessary or desirable to sell data on subscribers to third parties?

In North America the potential for abuse of personal data is made more serious because private-sector developments in information technology occur in an environment that is largely unregulated, particularly when it comes to the protection of privacy. Some attempts at industry self-regulation have been made, most notably the Warner Amex Code of Privacy, developed during the implementation of the QUBE two-way cable system in Columbus, OH. But the industry's response to privacy concerns has generally been inadequate.

THE FOCUS OF THIS BOOK

There is a tendency for any statutes and regulations involving new information technology to ignore issues of privacy and confidentiality. I prefer to assume that such continuing manifestations of insensitivity to privacy are inadvertent and that a process of consciousness-raising about privacy among both individuals and organizations will be successful in promoting greater concern. This book, among other things, attempts to demonstrate to the public, legislators and industry policymakers the need for a critical awareness of the inherent threats to privacy embodied in specific new technologies.

The chapters that follow take a close look at the prospects for invasion of personal privacy involved in interactive services and evaluate various remedies that already exist or are proposed. The recommendations and policy alternatives offered here identify the competing interests of subscribers, the cable industry, telephone companies, various levels of government and society as a whole.

This book favors a combined approach of industry and governmental regulation for the protection of personal privacy in interactive systems. My primary hope is that companies offering two-way services will self-regulate before additional government intervention, about which the industry is so critical, becomes necessary. Self-regulation at an early point in the development of any new form of information technology can be accomplished at minimal cost, especially in comparison to *ex post facto* attempts to patch on "solutions." Advance planning is particularly crucial to the design and configurations of software and hardware for interactive services. In addition, it is in the cable industry's best interest to address these issues now, before concerns about invasion of privacy become a significant barrier to consumer acceptance of two-way services. Fears raised by George Orwell's *Nineteen Eighty-Four* about the negative implications of advanced technology continue to this day. The threat of unfavorable media attention, which is sure to be drawn to any abuses of the confidentiality of subscriber information that might occur, should be an incentive for voluntary self-regulation.[1]

Although self-regulation has many advantages, it cannot solve all of the privacy problems involved in two-way services. As the Canadian Cable Television Association (CCTA) has indicated, as a trade association it "has limitations that do not extend beyond recommendation in what may ultimately be included in the business practices of its individual members." Government regulatory agencies will therefore have to monitor the progress of industry attempts at self-regulation and take appropriate steps to intervene if adequate self-regulation does not occur. Furthermore, government bodies should provide subscribers with legal recourse in case invasion of privacy does occur. Some issues, such as the regulation of third-party access to subscriber records, will probably require legislation. Whatever policies individual cable companies have in place, the legitimacy of and procedures for access by law enforcers and government agencies are beyond their power to establish.

This book does not emphasize the many positive aspects of two-way systems, but instead focuses on the risks users face in losing control of information about themselves as they make use of these desirable and beneficial services. I have purposely adopted a pro-privacy stance in order to alert cable and telephone companies, policymakers and the general public to the need for attention to privacy issues while two-way services are still at a design and pilot stage. Daily pressures in the competitive cable industry leave little time for considerations about the protection of privacy. The implications for personal privacy of new forms of technology are all too often ignored until there is public outcry. This usually only occurs in response to a particular controversy, such as the proposal of a national data bank in the U.S. in the mid-1960s,[2] or an episode like Watergate that flagrantly demands that the American public sit up and take notice.

Fortunately, the pace of introduction of two-way services furnishes a valuable opportunity for cable companies to pursue self-regulation and for government and regulatory agencies to ensure that the private sector is sensitive to the privacy interests of citizens. As Japanese expert Yoneji Masuda has envisioned the impact of the revolution in computer technology: "On the one hand, the completely automated state, the Orwellian nightmare, repression of individual rights. And on the other hand, fantastic new opportunities for human beings, a completely democratic, harmonious, living society. Both are equally possible."[3]

NOTES

1. Recent press treatment of two-way cable services include: Margaret Munro, "Cable TV's threat to privacy a growing concern," *The Ottawa Citizen,* January 19, 1983, p. 9 (syndicated in Southam newspapers across Canada); Robert Block, "Here's looking at you," *Canadian Lawyer,* November 1982, pp. 6, 9–10, 39; Peter Kerr, "How Can Privacy Be Safeguarded," *The New York Times,* December 13, 1983, p. 32H; and Daphne Lavers, "Subscriber Privacy in Two-Way Systems: Can 'Big Brother' be Kept at Bay?," *Cable Communications Magazine,* LI (March 1984), pp. 18–22.

2. See David H. Flaherty, *Privacy and Government Data Banks. An International Perspective* (London, U.K.: Mansell), pp. 21, 108–109, 264.

3. Interview, *Computerworld,* June 14, 1982, In-Depth, p. 6.

2

The Protection of Privacy

THE NATURE OF PRIVACY

In simple terms, concern for personal privacy involves an individual's basic desire to be left alone to enjoy a private life. People want to choose freely under what circumstances, and to what extent, they will reveal their attitudes and their behavior to others.[1]

Alan F. Westin, in *Privacy and Freedom* (1967), identified four integral states of privacy which, when taken together, add focus to the definition of the term. These are the concerns of an individual to enjoy solitude, initimacy, anonymity and reserve. Solitude, the most pristine form of privacy, refers to the individual's desire to be let alone without outside interference. Intimacy refers to the state of privacy that two friends, a husband and wife, or a family might want to enjoy together away from the outside world. Anonymity refers to a person's wish to be free of external surveillance. Finally, reserve refers specifically to an individual's desire to control the flow of information about himself or herself. All of these concerns have some relevance to the privacy interests at stake in using two-way services.

Arnold Simmel, in the *International Encyclopedia of the Social Sciences* (1968), ties together several of Westin's states of privacy in the following useful comment: "Privacy is a concept related to solitude, secrecy and autonomy, but it is not synonymous with these terms; for beyond the purely descriptive aspects of privacy as isolation from the company, the curiosity and the influence of others, privacy implies a normative element: the right to exclusive control to access to private realms." This last phrase has particular relevance to any household's right to regulate all forms of outside intrusion into the activities carried out and opinions expressed within a strictly private domain.

Two principal premises of this book are 1) that privacy is not an absolute value—it is in competition with other individual and collective values; and 2) that an individual in the late twentieth century can no longer adequately protect his or her own privacy without the assistance of regulatory authorities.

5

The first premise takes into account the fact that an individual may have to choose to relinquish some of his or her privacy in return for the benefits accrued from the use of services provided by an outside source, such as interactive cable. It is, of course, understood that the proliferation of new information systems poses no threat to those individuals to whom privacy is unimportant. In addition, what is considered private and personal information by one individual may not be looked on as such by another. Yet, although some people may willingly and consciously give up a certain amount of personal privacy in return for obvious benefits, it seems unlikely that more than a few individuals would completely sacrifice their personal privacy.

The second premise is examined later in this chapter in the discussion of data protection initiatives.

Public Concern About Privacy

While some individuals may place more value on privacy than others, recent studies have indicated that, on the whole, privacy is an issue of significant concern to the general public. Indeed, according to a May 1982 survey conducted by Bell Canada ("Public Attitudes Toward the New Micro-Electronic Technologies"), "privacy and confidentiality of personal information is the key public issue surrounding the spread of new technologies."

A Louis Harris survey, commissioned by the Southern New England Telephone Co. and reported in the December 8, 1983 *New York Times* found that the percentage of the general public "very concerned" about privacy threats had grown from 31% in 1978 to 48% by September 1983, when the telephone poll of 1256 persons was undertaken. In addition, some 84% of respondents believed that it would be easy for someone to assemble a master profile about them that would invade their privacy. A similar percentage favored criminal sanctions against data-collecting businesses that violated an individual's privacy.

The findings of the London Privacy Survey, which polled a random sample of 210 households in London, Ontario in 1982, also confirm the extent to which the general public is concerned about the preservation of its privacy; 90% of respondents cited the protection of privacy as important or very important. When compared to other major social and economic issues, the protection of privacy was rated as only slightly less important than controlling inflation, unemployment and crime, yet it was deemed more important than stopping the spread of nuclear weapons and ending strikes. Sixty-two percent of those polled were very concerned or somewhat concerned about the threats to their personal privacy in Canada today. Eighty-four percent agreed wholly or partially that storage of personal information on computers poses a danger to personal privacy, and 80% agreed or somewhat agreed that cable companies offering two-way services would have access to too much information about their personal lives. Survey results also indicate that people do not trust governments and the private sector to use personal information properly; 62% of the London respondents were concerned about how businesses used personal information solicited from them, while 49% expressed distrust about the federal and provincial governments' use of information.[2]

It should be mentioned here that individuals residing in different countries or even different regions of the same country have diverse opinions both as to the importance of privacy and about what personal information is regarded as sensitive. For the most part, Canadians and residents of the United Kingdom have been much less openly concerned to date about the protection of personal privacy than citizens in the United States, Sweden and West Germany.

When abuses of personal privacy are brought to public attention by newspapers or commissions of inquiry in Canada, for example, the degree of public outrage seems to be very muted or at best, short-lived. One result is that Canadian politicians have felt very little pressure to strengthen legislation for the protection of privacy, especially at the provincial level. However, there have been signs that this situation in Canada is changing. In the spring of 1982 the Quebec government passed legislation creating a data protection commission along European lines to regulate the public sector. In addition, in July 1982 the federal government passed a new and reinvigorated federal Privacy Act. In May 1984 the Ontario government hosted a symposium and interprovincial meeting, which concluded that the protection of personal information in both the public and private sectors has become an important issue.

Privacy, Voluntariness and Informed Consent

To date, there has been only limited recognition, especially under Canadian and English law, of the individual's *legal* right to privacy. Such non-legal status seems appropriate considering that the enjoyment of privacy will always be governed by personal preferences and the balancing of conflicting interests by each individual. While governments, law enforcers and courts may establish the limits of an individual's claim to privacy, the search for privacy should also touch on various non-legal concerns, such as the character of family, neighborhood and community life; communications and correspondence; and the effects of institutional life on individuals. Because privacy is such a broad and general concept and one defined on a personal, individualized basis, it is unlikely that it will achieve complete recognition as a legal and constitutional right, no matter how desirable that goal might seem to be.

Since under Canadian and American law people are for the most part left to their own devices when it comes to protecting their privacy, the issues of voluntariness and informed consent become essential elements in understanding and dealing with the potential dangers to privacy posed by the use of two-way services. A person can, for example, voluntarily choose whether to subscribe to two-way services, whether to limit the specific interactive services that are brought into the home, and whether to restrict the use of the system to what the individual regards as nonsensitive matters. If a person were to choose freely to subscribe to every available two-way service, with reasonable awareness of its implications for his or her personal privacy, one might question the person's judgment but could not claim that invasion of the person's privacy was occurring. There are, no doubt, some individuals who would have no objection to having their opinions on particular issues continually recorded or their TV viewing habits identified in detail. But individuals should be fully informed of the information being collected by companies offering two-way services and what is being done with it. With this end in mind, companies must adopt a standard code of fair information practices, which includes controls on the collection and transfer of personal information, and terms and conditions for the maintenance of data and the preservation of their security.

Because interactive cable services can collect information about individuals and their behavior within the confines of their own homes and often without their knowledge—e.g., the data available to cable company computers as a result of channel-monitoring capacity—they represent a heretofore unprecedented potential for violation of personal privacy and challenge the traditional concept that "a man's house is his castle."

As stated in a 1981 Collingwood Associates study for the U.S. Federal Trade Commission, "it is difficult for consumers to ever learn that their privacy has been breached. Again, consumers may not even know about the privacy implications of the services in the first place." The study added that "even if consumers had such information, they could do little as individuals to protect their privacy."[3]

Both the Collingwood Associates study and a 1982 Gardner and White study for the New York State Consumer Protection Board suggest that governments and companies have an obligation to educate consumers about the privacy risks of interactive services. There is, of course, a difference between educating and protecting consumers. In Canada, some consumer protection has generally been accepted as the responsibility of one level of government or another. Yet, except in the credit information field, few government initiatives have been taken with respect to the private sector protection of privacy. Gardner and White note that consumers become part of the problem because of their orientation to convenience and general insensitivity to privacy issues: "the privacy-convenience trade-off is a silent, invisible one. . . ."[4]

GOVERNMENT INITIATIVES IN DATA PROTECTION

The buildup of automated personal information systems has clearly made the protection of private life very difficult. The new media, which include everything from interactive cable television and telephone services to electronic newspapers and videotex services,[5] and the accompanying use of computers, microchip technology, and satellite and microwave communications are making possible the continued accumulation, storage, use and transfer of massive amounts of personal information on every aspect of life in modern industrial societies. This information about individuals must be kept appropriately confidential so that their personal privacy is upheld. The preservation of the confidentiality and security of personal information is called data protection; at present, it is the most pressing area of concern for the protection of privacy.

During the 1970s many European nations—Sweden, West Germany and France, in particular—created data protection laws and agencies to regulate the storage of personal information in both the public and private sectors, a process which is continuing in Western Europe during the 1980s.

In the United States, there is ongoing debate at the federal level as to whether Congress can continue to protect personal privacy on a sector-by-sector basis under the umbrella of the Privacy Act of 1974. The burden of fashioning specific new legislation to protect such data as medical records, and the nonexistence of any organization to articulate privacy interests on a continuing basis may eventually necessitate the creation of a federal Privacy Protection Commission in the United States.[6] Canada and its provinces did not establish agencies charged with general data protection until 1977; when the new Privacy Act came into effect on July 1, 1983, the office of the federal Privacy Commissioner assumed many of the characteristics of a European data protection commission. The province of Quebec has also created a European-style commission for data protection.[7]

The right to privacy has received only limited constitutional recognition in North America. While the U.S. Constitution does not explicitly state a right to privacy, the Supreme Court has, by process of judicial interpretation, concluded that a U.S. citizen's right to personal privacy is protected by the Constitution. In addition, the constitutions of several states, such as California and Florida, include provisions for the right to privacy. In Canada, however, no such constitutional right exists. The 1982 Canadian Charter of Rights and Freedoms does not include a right to privacy, and, on the whole, the protection of the legal right to personal privacy is hardly recognized in Canadian law.[8]

It is possible that a preexisting right to privacy might be judicially enforced in Canada on the basis of Article 26 of the federal Charter of Rights and Freedoms, which provides that the enumeration of certain rights and freedoms in the charter "shall not be construed as denying the existence of any other rights or freedoms that exist in Canada." But a carefully drafted constitutional amendment would be far more effective in guaranteeing the protection of Canadians' privacy. Although data protection will always require statutory intervention, a constitutional right to privacy could provide a general basis for claims a person might wish to assert against the private sector. Indicative of the Canadian government's reluctance to "legalize" privacy was the defeat of a motion to add "freedom from unreasonable interference with privacy, family, home, and correspondence" to the Canadian constitution at hearings before the Special Joint Committee of the Senate and House of Commons on the Constitution of Canada on January 22, 1981.[9] Although the New Democratic Party supported the proposal put forth by the Progressive Conservative party, a Liberal critic suggested that "the right to privacy" is "a concept that is too vague and ill-defined," and worried about how the courts would interpret this right.

U.S. Initiatives in Data Protection Legislation

As mentioned earlier, the U.S. has had more success to date than almost any other western nation in developing a constitutional basis for the right of privacy at both the federal and state levels. People try to assert legal claims to privacy for an enormous range of activities. American achievements in the restricted area of data protection are more limited. The main component of U.S. law affecting government record-keeping is the Privacy Act of 1974. State legislation in the form of fair information practice statutes also imposes limits on the kind of information that governments can collect and maintain about individuals.[10]

The most significant state statute is New York's Protection of Personal Privacy in Public Records Act, which took effect on September 1, 1984. The particular strength of the New York law is that it requires the state Committee on Open Government to act as an overseer to ensure its effective implementation.

Canada and the United States currently leave data collection activities in the private sector largely unregulated, except in such specialized areas as credit reporting. The U.S. Privacy Protection Study Commission made a number of recommendations for statutory changes in the private sector in its 1977 report, *Personal Privacy in an Information Society,* but these have had few results, largely because of the legislative failure of President Carter's privacy initiative in such areas as banking, insurance and medical records. Thus the U.S. continues to follow an *ad hoc* process of fashioning specialized solutions to data protection problems in the private sector, as is the case with the cable privacy initiatives discussed in Chapter 5.

Canadian Initiatives in Data Protection Legislation

The most important and relevant data protection legislation in Canada is the federal Privacy Act of 1982. This legislation supplanted the privacy provisions in Part IV of the Canadian Human Rights Act of 1977, which had introduced principles of fair information practice in the federal public sector and which had also created the post of Privacy Commissioner. While the Commissioner's activities under the old act were generally limited to responding to complaints from individuals, the 1982 act considerably strengthened the investigative powers of the office.

The new Privacy Act basically regulates the collection, retention, disposal, protection and disclosure of personal information by the federal government. Individuals with grievances can bring complaints to the Privacy Commissioner and ultimately, if denied access to their files, to the Federal Court of Canada. Although the Privacy Act does not apply to the private sector, the power of the Privacy Commissioner to carry out special investigations does extend to "persons or bodies, other than government institutions, that come within the legislative authority of Parliament."[11] Since cable television companies are generally subject to such authority, this provision would allow the Privacy Commissioner to undertake a study of privacy in two-way services and make recommendations to Parliament for appropriate protective measures.

Earlier in Canadian legislative history, the federal Protection of Privacy Act of 1974—although it legitimized wiretapping in the course of controlling the interception of private communications under the criminal law—did furnish for the first time some federal statutory recognition of the right to privacy.[12] Its relevance for the protection of privacy in two-way information systems would depend on whether or not it could be used to prosecute anyone intercepting a "private communication" sent over a coaxial cable.

In terms of provincial government support of privacy, Quebec became the only province to enact data protection legislation for the public sector when it passed Law 65 in June 1982.[13] (The first eight of the 180 articles in the Quebec law took effect on October 1, 1982; the provisions on data protection became effective on July 1, 1984.) The law incorporates the standard provisions for fair information practices usually found in data protection laws. Although the independent supervisory commission created under this law does not have regulatory powers over the private sector, the principles incorporated in the legislation can serve as a guide to private sector operations involving the collection and use of personal data; the commission could also draw attention to private sector privacy problems in one of its periodic reports to the Quebec government.

Quebec demonstrated its dedication to privacy in 1975 when it adopted the Quebec Charter of Human Rights and Freedoms; Article 5 of this influential charter guarantees that "every person has a right to respect for his private life."[14] But while residents of Quebec might be able to make a legal claim that certain practices involved in two-way services invaded their right of privacy, it is highly unlikely that any private citizen would initiate litigation based on this legal stipulation alone.

The existing provincial Privacy Acts in British Columbia (1968), Manitoba (1970) and Saskatchewan (1974), which make it a tort or civil wrong to violate the privacy of another—such as in the wrongful use of an individual's photograph for advertising purposes—are both relatively unused and unusable and, because of their limited scope and application, would be of no assistance in responding to challenges posed by the new information technology.[15] Although the framers of such legislation are to be commended for their attempts to provide civil recourse for invasion of privacy, the statutes are not the equivalent of data protection laws.

While the Ontario Commission on Freedom of Information and Individual Privacy did not specifically address detailed issues associated with new information technology in its excellent 1980 report entitled *Public Government for Private People,* it *did* provide a suitable framework for regulation by focusing on informational privacy. The Commission recommended the establishment of an administrative body, the Data Protection Authority, to apply statutory standards of fair information practices to the management of personal data systems in the public sector and to give advice on record-keeping practices in the private sector.[16]

In May 1984 the Ontario government finally introduced in the legislature a bill on Privacy and Access to Information. Since the bill has major structural inadequacies, it is unlikely to be enacted in its present form in the near future. Thus, there are currently no existing mechanisms in the province of Ontario that can be automatically used to regulate privacy protection for individuals in conjunction with new information technology such as interactive services.

CABLE INDUSTRY RESISTANCE TO PRIVACY REGULATION

There is some tendency in the cable industry to regard privacy as an issue of concern only for extremists, faddists and civil libertarians. The heavy involvement of cable companies in the capital-intensive phase of building and rebuilding their systems tends to relegate concern for social issues such as privacy to the back burner. In addition, under one-way cable systems privacy was not a problem industry participants had to confront. Because of the proliferation of two-way services, however, cable companies now need to bring the same level of sophisticated consideration to privacy issues as they have to their technical and financial needs.

Among the arguments put forth by some cable company spokesmen denying the need for privacy protection are the ideas that subscribers have to trust the companies, that no privacy problems currently exist, that privacy is not a pressing issue for subscribers, that subscribing to cable is a voluntary act and that cable companies are just common carriers.

In general, cable companies are resistant to any further regulation by government authorities and therefore shun government intervention on behalf of privacy protection. Cable companies in Canada believe they are already operating under a substantial regulatory burden, especially in comparison to their American counterparts. A number of cable industry participants also feel that there is no need to legislate morality when it comes to such issues as the protection of privacy. (The contrasting opinion, held by radical sociologists, for example, is that the private sector will never decide "to do good," unless forced to do so.)

Reliance on the Marketplace

A popular viewpoint is that because cable companies have to rely on the goodwill of subscribers to stay in business, they would not want to jeopardize consumer trust by misuse of personal information. But this assertion does not deal with the economically motivated possibility that at some point a cable company may decide to sell personal information for profit. Indeed, cable companies, currently under considerable pressure to improve their marketing functions, are recruiting marketing and advertising specialists who may quite soon become aware of the monetary value of identifiable data on consumers collected from subscribers to two-way cable services.[17] It therefore becomes easy to believe that, as suggested by a recent report to the New York State Consumer Protection Board, reliance on the marketplace as a form of privacy protection is an obsolete and simplistic notion.[18]

In addition, almost no legal restrictions exist at present to prevent a cable company from selling personal information in its possession, since the general view in North America is that such data belong to the company itself. In Canada, however, the CRTC regulates all aspects of a "broadcasting receiving undertaking" (the legal term for a local cable company), and it could therefore interfere with any attempt to sell subscriber data to generate income. Since the U.S. does not regulate cable in the same way, there are no legal prohibitions on a local cable company selling personal data, unless there is a municipal ordinance or a cable privacy statute to the contrary. (See Chapter 5.)

Specific Cable Company Contentions

Local cable companies point to the fact that the amount of subscriber information they already collect has given them some experience in the protection of privacy. One local cable company in Canada, for example, automatically turns down all requests for information on particular subscribers. Calls requesting such information are directed to the attention of management and subscriber information files are kept locked.

Of course, the simple fact that a person is a subscriber to basic cable is not, by itself, sensitive information. Cable companies currently have more detailed information only on those subscribers who rent costly equipment such as converters from them; in that case, the cable company's files might contain such credit information as where a subscriber worked and banked and his or her payment history. But the crucial point is that the amount and nature of personal information that will be generated by the use of interactive services will differ significantly from and be of far greater magnitude than data collected under existing practices. Thus, present cable company standards on confidentiality may partially result from their lack of information useful for marketing purposes.

Another position cable companies are taking is that privacy is simply not a pressing issue and that it would be premature to do anything about it. This attitude essentially characterizes the initial response of several national or provincial groups such as the National Cable Television Association, the Canadian Cable Television Association and the Ontario Cable Television Association. While individual cable companies, their industry associations and regulatory bodies will have to determine whether or not privacy is a matter to be dealt with at this point in time, this volume urges that the time to plan for the protection of privacy is *now,* before more sensational stories appear in the press to discourage consumers and before technical and software designs for interactive systems are completed. If cable companies do not voluntarily decide to deal with the issue of personal privacy, it will not be difficult (especially given the current developments in American states described in Chapter 5) for privacy advocates to persuade legislators and regulators at the federal, state and provincial levels to initiate action that will ensure the protection of personal privacy in all types of interactive systems.

Cable companies also argue that those subscribing to cable services do so on a voluntary basis. But, as already discussed, the voluntariness of participation in an interactive service does not automatically ensure the protection of privacy, because a significant part of the information derived from subscribers in a two-way system is collected automatically, at any moment and without the individual's knowledge.

A final argument put forth by cable companies is that even if someone could coordinate personal information derived from all of the possible interactive cable services, it would not be the cable company that would do so, since it is only a carrier or transporter of personal information. Such an argument does not hold water considering the current state of cable regulation in Canada and the United States; nor do most cable companies want to be regulated as common carriers. (A detailed discussion of this topic appears in

Chapter 7.) The issue of whether a cable or telephone company has any responsibility for the confidentiality of personal information in cases where a third party delivers a commercial service over the medium only complicates and adds urgency to the need to fashion measures to protect consumer privacy in all interactive services.

Similarities to Other Industries

Cable companies contend that they are no different from other private businesses that collect personal information, such as credit card and telephone companies, who face similar problems with respect to confidentiality. This is a valid argument, to some extent, and one which serves as a useful reminder that all two-way services pose significant privacy problems, whether delivered over coaxial cable, telephone wires or via fiber optics. It is therefore quite appropriate to take an integrated approach to solving the problems of protecting privacy, confidentiality and security in all forms of interactive services. But, as is illustrated in Chapter 4, the privacy problems inherent in interactive services are much greater than any previously encountered in the use of traditional telephone or cable services.

It is nevertheless helpful to examine the potential threats to privacy posed by the use of telephone services, as many of these are similar to those encountered in the use of interactive cable. The telephone is a two-way system that enters almost every North American home. Transmissions that occur on the telephone are subject to legal and illegal wiretaps. Eavesdropping is also possible by third parties, including company personnel. Long-distance calls via satellites can be readily intercepted, especially by national security agencies.[19] In addition, the telephone company may monitor conversations as part of its regular work and it maintains long-distance billing records, which specify numbers called. Moreover, the existence of the telephone in the home makes possible intrusive and unwanted telephone calls.

Fortunately, telephone companies have taken a number of steps toward the protection of privacy (which are discussed in Chapter 7), and their efforts at self-regulation can serve as a model for cable companies. But in spite of these measures, the degree to which privacy can be violated provides compelling arguments for external regulation of both cable and telephone companies for the protection of confidentiality.

Credit card companies also possess a great deal of personal information about cardholders. The record of a credit card purchase can in fact establish the presence and activities of a given consumer at a particular place on a particular date, and such data may be recorded in a computerized cardholder file shortly after the transaction has been completed. Current billing processes are being handled with ever greater frequency in an online mode, so that a company like American Express, for example, is immediately notified about a credit charge through an automated point-of-sale device that also authorizes the transaction, or receives the charge data at the end of a business day through direct links between the computers of a retail operation and those of the credit card company. Thus, existing credit card systems also have considerable unregulated capacity for invading the privacy of individuals.

It must be kept in mind that, along with the similarities we have just examined, there are some substantial differences between the cable industry and other industries. The most significant of these for our purposes is that, because it is financially less secure than telephone and credit card companies, the cable industry may find itself under more economic pressure to sell information about subscribers.

Lack of Demonstrated Abuses

An issue frequently debated in connection with data protection for any type of information system is the extent to which abuses of personal privacy need to be demonstrated before regulation should occur. In the Collingwood Associates study for the Federal Trade Commission, the authors analyzed Warner Amex's QUBE operation in Columbus and concluded, "We did not identify any breaches of privacy—only the potential for such breaches."

Yet, a lack of concrete evidence of abuses of personal information does not obviate the need for regulation. The Watergate experience in the U.S. and certain data collection practices by the security services of the RCMP in Canada[20] indicate the extent to which the potential for data abuse may become reality. Because neither the government nor the private sector has any incentives to be candid and forthcoming about such matters, consumers generally are unlikely to know the extent to which their personal privacy has in fact been invaded.

Perhaps the best response to this argument against self-regulation or external regulation is found in the results of the inquiry by the Royal Commission on the Confidentiality of Health Records in Ontario. Under the direction of Mr. Justice Horace Krever, the Commission had the power to subpoena individuals in the public and private sectors to compel them to testify about their current information practices and had the staff to investigate abuses. The Commission found that supposedly confidential health-care data on individuals were being disclosed in an unauthorized manner to certain physicians, law enforcers, lawyers and private investigative services.[21]

SELF-REGULATION BY CABLE COMPANIES

Although their motives may sometimes be questionable, cable companies are not totally unconcerned about the protection of privacy. They are aware of the potentially explosive nature of the privacy issue, especially through discussions arising at American municipal franchise hearings at which the public has voiced its sentiments. Because they know that problems of protecting privacy and confidentiality could become a barrier to the introduction of interactive services if unresolved, cable companies cannot ignore the issue completely.

Thus, some concern for the privacy interests of consumers does motivate North American cable companies, even if the motive may be purely economic. In *Electronic Nightmare* (1981), John Wicklein notes that profit is the only concern of commercial television executives and it would be naive to expect cable companies to be run as philanthropic enterprises. Nevertheless, far-sighted executives are taking the issue seriously. The study by Collingwood Associates previously referred to reported that "the QUBE system managers do see the protection of privacy as in their self-interest, since all revenues are derived from consumers at this time."[22] In addition, senior management at both Rogers Cablesystems and Maclean Hunter recognizes that it is appropriate for cable companies to be exploring ways to protect privacy now.

The most significant action taken by a cable company in recognition of the privacy problems inherent in interactive cable services was the November 1981 publication by Warner Amex Cable Communications Inc. of its Code of Privacy. Warner Amex's Code of Privacy specifies that the cable company will keep subscribers informed of its information-gathering activities and sets out the terms under which information about subscribers will be used (primarily for billing and subscriber services). In the opinion of Gustave M. Hauser, then chairman of Warner Amex, the company's experience "demonstrates that two-way cable communications and protection of individual rights are thoroughly compatible. It is clearly possible to provide subscribers with the important benefits of interactive cable, while at the same time guarding against real or perceived infringements of their individual rights."[23] The Warner Amex Code (see Appendix) and other cable industry attempts at self-regulation are discussed in detail in Chapters 5 and 7.

On the whole, the current level of response of American and Canadian cable companies to the question of the protection of the privacy and confidentiality of subscriber data is generally inadequate. One goal of this volume is to assist companies offering interactive services in clarifying their thinking about the issue of privacy and in preparing appropriate responses to identifiable problems. Among the recommendations we propose is that each company anticipating the introduction of two-way systems should have policies on privacy and confidentiality already in place. Except for one Canadian cable company which has already drafted policies on subscriber privacy, the major multi-system operators in Canada have made no such provisions, even though every major Canadian MSO already has equipment that is capable of monitoring individual information interactively. Furthermore, as in measures already undertaken by telephone companies, company handbooks for employees should set forth explicit policies on confidentiality. Of course, these are just preliminary suggestions; detailed discussions of further recommendations can be found in Chapters 5 and 7.

NOTES

1. See Alan F. Westin, *Privacy and Freedom* (New York: Atheneum, 1967), p. 7.

2. Neil J. Vidmar, "Privacy and Two-Way Cable Television: A Study of Canadian Public Opinion." (Downsview, Ontario: Ontario Ministry of Transportation and Communications, May 1983), pp. 15–16, 27, 37, 43 and table 4.

3. Deanna Collingwood Nash and John B. Smith, *Interactive Home Media and Privacy.* Prepared for the Office of Policy Planning, U.S. Federal Trade Commission (Washington, DC: Collingwood Associates, Inc., January 1981), pp. 12, 14.

4. *Ibid.,* p. 17. Sidney L. Gardner and Robin White, *New Technology and the Right to Privacy: State Responses to Federal Inaction. A Report to the New York State Consumer Protection Board.* (Unpublished draft, August 1982), pp. 6–8.

5. See, for example, Swedish Ministry of Education and Culture, *New Media. Broadcast Teletext, Videotex.* (Summary of the final report presented by the Commission on New Information Technology, Stockholm, Sweden, 1981); and Efrem Sigel et al., *The Future of Videotext: Worldwide Prospects for Home/Office Electronic Information Services* (White Plains, NY: Knowledge Industry Publications, Inc., 1983).

6. See David H. Flaherty, "The Need for an American Privacy Protection Commission," *Government Information Quarterly,* I, 1984, pp. 235–258.

7. An Act to enact the Access to Information Act and the Privacy Act, S.C. 1980-81-82, c. 111; an Act respecting access to documents held by public bodies and the protection of personal information, S.Q., 1982, c. 30.

8. See Peter T. Burns, "The Law and Privacy: The Canadian Experience," *Canadian Bar Review,* LIV, 1976, pp. 1–64, and Burns, "Privacy and the Common Law: A Tangled Skein Unravelling?" in Dale Gibson, ed., *Aspects of Privacy Law* (Toronto: Butterworths, 1980), pp. 21–40. See also H. Patrick Glenn, "The Right to Privacy in Quebec Law," in Gibson, ed., *Aspects of Privacy Law,* pp. 42–71.

9. The debate can be followed in *Minutes of Proceedings and Evidence of the Special Joint Committee of the Senate and the House of Commons on the Constitution of Canada,* January 22, 1981, Issue No. 43, pp. 7, 55–56.

10. See Robert Aldrich, *Privacy Protection Law in the United States,* NTIA Report 82-98 (Washington, DC: U.S. Department of Commerce, May 1982).

11. An Act to enact the Access to Information Act and the Privacy Act, S.C. 1980-81-82, c. 111, s. 60(1)(c).

12. S.C. 1973-4, c. 50, as amended.

13. An Act respecting access to documents held by public bodies and the protection of personal information, S.Q. 1982, c. 30.

14. Glenn, "The Right to Privacy in Quebec Law," p. 42.

15. Burns, "The Law and Privacy," pp. 32–39; and Philip H. Osborne, "The Privacy Acts of British Columbia, Manitoba and Saskatchewan," in Gibson, ed., *Aspects of Privacy Law* (Toronto: Butterworths, 1980), pp. 73–110.

16. Ontario, *Public Government for Private People. The Report of the Commission on Freedom of Information and Individual Privacy/1980* (3 vols., Toronto, 1980), III, 680–82, 732-40.

17. *The New York Times,* August 17, 1983, p. D15, and December 13, 1983, p. H32.

18. Gardner and White, *New Technology and the Right to Privacy,* pp. 36–47.

19. See James Bamford, *The Puzzle Palace. A Report on America's Most Secret Agency* (Boston, MA: Houghton Mifflin, 1982), Chapter 5; and *The Manchester Guardian Weekly,* November 21, 1982, pp. 4–5.

20. Nash and Smith, *Interactive Home Media and Privacy,* p. 10; and Commission of Inquiry Concerning Certain Activities of the Royal Canadian Mounted Police, *Freedom and Security Under the Law, Second Report* (2 vols., Ottawa, August 1981), pp. 221–76, 781–812, 829–38.

21. Ontario, *Report of the Commission of Inquiry into the Confidentiality of Health Information* (3 vols., Toronto, 1980).

22. John Wicklein, *Electronic Nightmare: The New Communications and Freedom* (New York: The Viking Press, 1979), p. 145; and Nash and Smith, *Interactive Home Media and Privacy*, p. 10.

23. Warner Amex Cable Communications, Inc., *Code of Privacy* (New York, 1981), Introduction.

3

The North American Cable Television Industry

CABLE TELEVISION IN THE UNITED STATES—OVERVIEW

Cable television in the U.S. evolved from community antenna television (CATV), a system used to deliver commercial television signals to remote rural areas which, because of distance from transmitting stations or mountainous terrain, could not previously receive such signals. Cable did not spread rapidly in its early years primarily because of prohibitive FCC regulations; the major impetus to its growth came in 1975 when Home Box Office (which had been involved in pay services since the early 1970s) switched from microwave to satellite transmission, thus becoming the first cable network with national reach. During the early 1980s multiple-system operators (MSOs) competed frantically for franchises to wire major urban and suburban areas; many of them promised interactive capability in order to win franchises. At the same time, the cable industry witnessed a tremendous upsurge of basic, advertiser-supported cable programming networks as well as premium pay channels.

From January 1980 to January 1984, the total number of cable subscribers in the U.S. (basic and pay) rose from 21.5 million to 60.1 million. Basic cable subscribers more than doubled, increasing from 15.8 million to 32.1 million within that period, while at the same time pay subscriptions grew from 5.7 million to 28 million. As of October 1983, about 71.2% of all U.S. TV households were passed by cable with slightly over 50% of these homes actually subscribing to basic cable. As of January 1982, 55,000 homes received two-way services, a figure which grew to some 350,000 subscribers by June 1984. Subscribers to teletext systems or to Viewtron rose from 33,500 to 190,000 within the same period.[1] And, according to a Paul Kagan Associates, Inc. survey, cable industry revenues for 1983 were an estimated $6 billion.

Because the subscriber figure of 50% of cable-capable homes has remained relatively constant within the past few years, most MSOs now realize that future growth must come from expansion within their systems; one element in this expansion for some MSOs is the development and marketing of interactive services.

CABLE TELEVISION IN CANADA

Cable television began in Canada in the early 1950s as a means of delivering improved reception of television signals. The first systems were in London, Ontario. Providing access to U.S. channels was a major reason for the rapid growth of cable service, making Canada one of the most heavily cabled countries in the world. Between 1973 and 1982 the number of operating cable systems increased from 362 to 564 and the number of total households passed by cable grew from 59.3% to 80%. Subscribers as a percentage of households passed by cable grew from 57% to 74.7% in the same period.

Pay television only began in Canada in the first months of 1983 and has been growing slowly. Less than 10% of the almost 5 million cable television subscribers were also pay TV subscribers as of October 31, 1983.[2]

MAJOR U.S. MULTIPLE SYSTEM OPERATORS (MSOs)

As of June 1984, the six leading multiple system operators (MSOs) in the United States accounted for a combined total of 21.4 million basic and pay cable units. They served 33.6% of all U.S. cable homes for a total of close to 11.5 million basic subscribers and 34.4% of pay cable units with some 9.9 million pay subscriptions.[3]

Tele-Communications Inc., with a total of 4.7 million basic and pay units—comprised of 2.8 million basic and 1.9 million pay—was the top U.S. MSO as of June 1984.[4] These figures include units under ownership as well as units under management that belong to TCI's partnerships with Taft Broadcasting (TCI/Taft), with Knight-Ridder (TKR Cable) and with Scripps (Telescripps). TCI, which operates in 43 states, is continuing to expand existing systems as well as acquire new ones. In the spring of 1983 the company established the TCI Addressable Center in Denver which enabled it to introduce addressability in over 150 of its systems. TCI revenues rose from $84.5 million in 1979 to $347.3 million in 1983, with operating income rising from $20.6 million to $84.5 million, but net earnings decreased from $28.9 million to $20.5 million within the same period.[5]

The second largest MSO, American Television and Communications Corp. (ATC), is part of Time Inc.'s Video Group; Time also owns Home Box Office and Cinemax. As of January 1984 ATC had a total of 4.6 million combined basic and pay subscriptions—2.4 million basic and 2.2 million pay.[6] In 1983 its systems served subscribers in 464 municipalities in 31 states. Some of its systems have two-way capability and offer interactive services. In 1983 it was granted the franchise for the western part of Queens, NY containing 250,000 households. Video Group revenues (which include Home Box Office and Cinemax as well as ATC) increased from $272 million in 1979 to nearly $1.1 billion in 1983, with income from continuing operations rising during that time from $68 million to $215 million.[7]

Group W Cable, owned by Westinghouse, is the third largest MSO and operates 150 systems in 34 states. Its combined basic and pay subscriptions totaled about 3.6 million in June 1984, with 2 million of these basic and 1.6 million pay.[8] In 1983 "Group W increased the number of subscribers, franchise wins and revenues while continuing major investments to upgrade its cable systems for future growth." Financial figures for Westinghouse's Broadcasting and Cable segment, of which Group W Cable is part, indicate an increase of revenues from $431.9 million in 1981 to $852.4 million in 1983, with operating profit declining from $76.4 million to $47.8 million in the same period. The building of new systems and upgrading of old ones, as well as the start-up costs of new cable program services have resulted in heavy expenditures for Group W in the last few years.[9]

The fourth largest U.S. MSO as of June 1984 was Cox Cable whose 3.1 million subscription units are made up of 1.5 million basic and 1.6 million pay,[10] making it the only major MSO whose pay-to-basic ratio is above 100%. Cox Cable, part of Cox Communications, had 54 wholly or majority owned cable systems in 23 states by year-end 1983. Cable television revenues for Cox rose from $90.9 million in 1979 to $337.4 million in 1983, while operating income for those years increased from $21.8 million to $45.4 million.[11]

With 1.4 million basic and 1.4 million pay subscribers as of March 1984, Storer Cable was the fifth leading MSO in June 1984.[12] While the company had been actively acquiring new franchises through 1982, it is now concentrating on marketing newly built systems and introducing new cable services. It is also selling and trading cable systems, or "clustering," in an effort to realize the efficiencies of administering geographically contiguous systems and to divest itself of systems where the expected rate of return on invested capital will take longer to achieve. Part of Storer Communications, Storer's Cable Communications Division, which operates in 170 locations, saw revenues grow from $132.8 million in 1981 to $291.1 million in 1983, although net income decreased during that time from $31.9 million to a net loss of $39.7 million.[13]

Warner Amex Cable Communications Inc., jointly owned by Warner Communications and American Express, was the sixth largest MSO in June 1984 with nearly 2.6 million subscriptions—about 1.4 million basic and 1.2 million pay.[14] Warner Amex operates 119 systems in 25 states and is also intent on moving from the acquisition of new franchises to completing current commitments and developing system clusters. Its interactive QUBE system in Columbus, OH and other cities (QUBE is discussed in detail in Chapter 4) is now focusing on network specials, local programming and pay-per-view. The Columbus QUBE system offers security services, opinion-polling and tele-education; it plans a telebanking service in the future and is developing two-way capacity for teleshopping, as is Cox Cable's Indax. Revenues for 1983 for Warner Amex (which also includes the two basic cable services, MTV:Music Television and Nickelodeon, provided by the Warner Amex Satellite Entertainment Co.) were $438 million, with a pretax loss of $150 million and a net loss of $99 million for that year.[15]

MAJOR CANADIAN MULTIPLE-SYSTEM OPERATORS (MSOs)

Three major cable television companies supply service to 80% of all Canadian cable television subscribers: Rogers Cablesystems Inc., Le Groupe Videotron and Maclean Hunter Cable TV Limited. These companies are multiple-system operators (MSOs) in that they control systems in a number of localities across the country, as do their American counterparts. There are 23 separate MSOs in Canada, but several are owned by Rogers or Telecable Videotron. Eight of these have a total of less than 25,000 subscribers.[16] In addition, although there are almost 600 licensed cable television companies operating in local communities, less than 100 have even 10,000 subscribers. Indeed, only 24 local Canadian cable systems have more than 50,000 subscribers.

As there are many differences between the interests of the large MSOs and the smaller companies, the Canadian cable television industry has been difficult to organize. These differences are accentuated by the disparity between the kinds of cable services that a large MSO can offer and the limited services available in the immediate future from most small local cable companies. Because it is unlikely that the smaller companies will become involved with the delivery of interactive services within the next several years, this volume focuses primarily on the activities of the major MSOs in both the U.S. and Canada.

A major Canadian MSO and one of the largest cable television companies in the world, Rogers Cablesystems serves 1.8 million cable subscribers in Canada, the United States and Ireland. The Canadian systems are heavily concentrated in urban centers in Ontario (10 franchises) and British Columbia-Alberta (3 franchises), including 353,969 subscribers in Toronto and 247,202 in Vancouver. Systems owned by Rogers have one-quarter of all cable subscribers in Canada. Rogers Cablesystems Inc. operates its Canadian systems through Canadian Cablesystems Ltd., which includes Premier Cablesystems Inc. in British Columbia and Alberta and Rogers Cable TV Ltd. in Ontario.[17]

Rogers has enjoyed tremendous growth in Canada and the U.S. during the last several years. But while assets rose from $126 million Canadian dollars in 1979 to $914 million in fiscal 1983, debt grew from $15 million in 1979 to $637 million in 1983, almost seven times the asset growth rate. While revenues continued to climb, the company reported a net loss of $15.1 million in fiscal 1983, as opposed to net income of $9.8 million in fiscal 1979, a situation which puts Rogers under substantial financial pressure. For the first nine months of fiscal 1984, Rogers lost $20 million.[18]

Two aggressive, fast-growing Canadian cable companies, Telecable Videotron Ltee. and Cablevision Nationale Ltee., are the two largest MSOs in Quebec. They are controlled by Le Groupe Videotron Ltee., making it the number two cable company in Canada (and among the largest in the world) with approximately 543,458 subscribers in 1983 and a gross income of $75 million for 1982. Its primary markets are the areas around Montreal and Quebec City. In the province of Quebec, Videotron serves 51% of all cable subscribers. Under the leadership of Andre Chagnon, it has vigorously pursued growth through acquisitions and major technological innovations.[19]

Maclean Hunter Cable TV Ltd. is the third largest MSO in Canada, with 352,805 subscribers in 16 Ontario systems. The cable company is a subsidiary of Maclean Hunter Limited, a diversified communications conglomerate which also owns magazines, television and radio stations, and related operations.[20] In 1983 cable television revenue was $115.1 million, an increase of 24% over the previous year.

A total of seven Canadian MSOs have cable holdings in the United States. Rogers and Maclean Hunter have 83% of the 825,000 American subscribers served by Canadian companies. Through Rogers U.S. Cablesystems Inc., Rogers has a 76% interest in local cable systems serving 159,000 subscribers in four primary clusters, including Portland, Minneapolis, San Antonio and southern California. After the division of assets of Rogers UA Cablesystems Inc., Rogers Cablesystems of America, Inc. owned additional U.S. systems serving some 307,000 subscribers at the end of fiscal 1983. Maclean Hunter provides services to 219,404 subscribers in one area of New Jersey and seven in Michigan. The remaining five Canadian MSOs operating in the U.S. are Cablecasting Ltd. (Georgia and California), Selkirk Communications Ltd. (Florida), Cablenet Ltd. (Illinois), Standard Broadcasting Corp. Ltd. (California) and Moffat Communications Ltd. (Texas and Florida).[21]

THE NORTH AMERICAN CABLE TELEVISION INDUSTRY TODAY

Intent on dealing with problems involving capital financing, strong competition, expansion, the introduction of pay television (in Canada), the search for new services and the challenge from conglomerates, the cable television industry in the U.S. and Canada faces a far less optimistic future than the one anticipated several years ago. In May 1980 at the annual meeting of the Canadian Cable Television Association in Vancouver, glowing prospects were predicted for cable companies during the 1980s.[22] But already by August 1982 the Canadian *Cable Communications Magazine* presented the following picture of the state of the North American cable industry:

> Its strengths include controlling the only broadband wire into the home, being able to pull large revenue streams out of homes, and having increasing financial resources; its weaknesses include falling profits due to intense franchise competition, municipal meddling, being forced to build more franchises than it would like, uncertainty over how to develop new businesses like security and business and data communications, lack of R and D capabilities, being forced to lay coaxial cable despite cost and performance advantages of fiber optics, and Hollywood's shortage of good programming.

By January 17, 1984 *The Boston Globe* editorialized that a nationwide illness was afflicting the cable television industry: "As a business investment, cable is looking less like a lean, profitable tiger and more like a lumbering white elephant."

Pay Cable in Canada

At present Canadian cable companies are heavily involved in the promotion of pay television, which began with considerable fanfare in February 1983. At the time, many industry observers and participants predicted a lucrative future for pay television in Canada, and the initial acceptance level on the part of the Canadian public exceeded expectations. But the overall experience of the first eighteen months demonstrates that the success of the new services was, for the most part, short-lived. In fact, of the seven pay service participants that started up services in February 1983, only two remain; they are now offering a single monopolistic service with each company controlling a separate part of Canada. Although major marketing campaigns are continuing, penetration rates nationally remain below 12%, and there is general agreement that the market for pay cable in Canada was simply overestimated.

The introduction of pay television involves substantial capital expenditures for cable companies, especially in Canada. It is very expensive to rebuild at least some of the hardware in local cable systems in order to provide pay television services. Although the Canadian cable companies are licensed by the CRTC in all aspects of their operations, it is not yet clear how they will be able to charge for pay television and other services. The CRTC continues to hold hearings on what is known as "tiering," which basically means how the cable companies structure their various cable services for sale to the consumer and for charging purposes. The packaging of special services offered separately from regular cable offerings could become an important source of new revenue for cable companies. Currently, cable users in Canada pay only one fee, but cable operators want to be able to "tier" their services so that subscribers pay for what they use, as is the case in the U.S. The CRTC has announced its willingness to accept proposals for programming to be carried on such cable television tiers.

Several decisions announced by the CRTC on January 5, 1984 were designed to reduce the regulatory burden on pay TV. Subsequent announcements of the CRTC, under its new chairman, Andre Bureau, indicated a "desire to keep regulation to a minimum," which has encouraged the cable television and pay TV companies about the future.[23]

Although pay television does not require two-way capability, there is a direct technological relationship between the introduction of addressable technology and the offering of various new services in the future. Once the necessary technology is in place, it will be more feasible to introduce various kinds of non-programming services.

Financial Problems Confronting the Cable Industry

The major cable companies in Canada are operating under a significant financial burden due to recent expansion, the need for capital to finance new services and the generally weak state of the economy. In general, it will be extremely expensive to update the physical plant, much of which is quite old. This particular problem does not exist in the U.S., where cable is very new.

The cable companies need a substantially increased transmission capacity, plus new amplifiers and splitters; these represent hefty expenses at a time when many companies are already heavily in debt and carrying a high interest load. If cable television has traditionally been viewed as an easy way to make money, this has not been true in recent years. An article in *The Globe and Mail* on June 3, 1982 quoted Rogers' vice president of finance as stating that the cable companies would need $100 million in capital in 1982 to maintain or update their systems. In 1984 that figure is considerably greater. Since cable companies finance half their loans through bank debt, they have had to pay banks and insurance companies high interest rates, even to raise enough capital to introduce pay television.

The cable television industry in the U.S. is also facing difficult economic times. Some of the reasons are similar to those that prevail in Canada. Pay TV services are not as successful as predicted, and only a few of the companies offering these services, led by Home Box Office and Showtime/The Movie Channel, are making money. Even though the base of cable subscribers is expanding rapidly, there is no longer a realistic expectation that 50 or 75 channels will eventually become available. Basic cable program services are being cut back, and cable companies find themselves unable to deliver certain services in their local franchises.[24]

Competition from Other Delivery Systems

Cable companies are increasingly confronting stiff competition from other technologies. Relying on coaxial cable as its basic delivery medium, cable is competing against industries relying on telephone lines, fiber optics and satellite transmissions. (A cable company could in fact employ any of these technologies.) Although cable's broadband capacities have considerable advantages over the narrowband characteristics of telephone wires, fiber optics offers even greater improvements in reaching individual homes. For example, the plans for wiring Britain, encouraged by the government of Prime Minister Thatcher, involve using fiber optic cables for the trunk lines and coaxial cables only at stations servicing 50,000 to 100,000 homes.[25]

In Canada the competition between Bell Canada and the cable companies to deliver interactive services to subscribing households could become extremely intense. At the CCTA convention in Vancouver in May 1980, Jerome Redican, a senior partner of the Canada Consulting Group, asserted:

> It would be foolhardy to think that cable can compete head to head with telephone companies. They can easily clobber an undercapitalized competitor for new services. They have the economic muscle, with annual new investments of about two billion—more than three times the total existing cable investment. And they have a paramount public policy position, providing an essential service that can justifiably claim protection.[26]

Similar competition exists in the U.S., where AT&T and the newly independent Bell operating companies are looking for opportunities in the cable television marketplace and in home information systems. In a classic example of converging technologies, Chesapeake & Potomac Telephone Co., a subsidiary of Bell Atlantic, is planning to build cable transport lines for a District of Columbia cable television system.[27]

The technology for a number of first-generation interactive services involves combining cable and telephone systems. In part because of the technical advantages of cable over telephone wires, cable companies are optimistic that they will win out over telephone companies in the race toward the wired society, but economic realities are necessitating some cooperation between the two industries in the early stages.

Cable companies also face competition from direct broadcast satellites which beam programming directly into a receiving dish or an earth station at a specific location. Canadian companies cannot put U.S. satellite communications on their standard cable services without permission from the CRTC. A greater threat is posed by the loss of multiple customers in an apartment house, condominium or hotel; a number of these use a satellite dish or purchase a transmission from a master antenna television operator.

A further aspect of the competitive situation facing major Canadian MSOs is that in recent years they have expanded considerably into the highly deregulated cable television market in the U.S. As mentioned earlier in this chapter both Rogers and Maclean Hunter have significant franchises in the U.S. In order to win these franchises the companies have had to make major promises, especially as regards the introduction of interactive services in newly wired communities. This process has proven to be very expensive, and some slowdown has occurred recently in the pace of wiring American cities. In fact, all cable companies operating in the U.S. have encountered technical and financial difficulties which are hindering the delivery of "franchise-driven" promises of two-way services.

Ownership of Cable Companies

An important aspect of the North American cable industry, which has meaningful implications for personal privacy, concerns the extent to which the leading multiple-system operators are independent companies as opposed to being parts of larger conglomerates. This issue has particular relevance to the confidentiality of identifiable personal information gathered by interactive cable services. Although an independent company like Rogers owns 14 cable systems in Canada, each operates locally and individually, sharing only the Rogers name. One advantage of such a setup is that it promotes decentralized information-handling activities and thus misuse of the data can only occur on a local basis. There appear to be few incentives for the interlinking of the various individual personal information systems of a large company such as Rogers, although it can be argued that it might be easier to regulate a large single system. Real and significant privacy risks for the individual could emerge from the integrated computer operation of large cable companies owning multiple systems, or from cable companies pooling data with other firms, such as those involved in communications, credit, banking, computer hardware manufacturing and the provision of information.

The risks to personal privacy through the sharing of personal information increase significantly if cable companies are taken over by larger information companies, such as retailers, publishers, or entertainment firms. In the U.S. a number of cable companies are owned by larger conglomerates. Time Inc., for example, owns both Home Box Office, the leading pay cable service, and American Television and Communications Corp., the second largest U.S. MSO with 2.4 million basic subscribers. Warner Amex Cable Communications Inc., which owns the QUBE system in Columbus, OH, could potentially share QUBE-obtained information about individuals with its owners, Warner Communications Inc. and American Express.[28]

The Federal Communications Commission in the United States has proposed to drop its rule prohibiting TV networks from owning cable companies.

This would just intensify problems of conglomerate control. In testimony before a committee of the New York State Assembly considering the future of cable television, Norma Rollins of the New York Civil Liberties Union argued strongly in favor of subscribers' privacy interests, stating:

> A look at the evolving corporate structures in our society is convincing evidence that cable television companies are very likely to be parts of. . .vast and varied conglomerate structures, and the exchange of information between its parts could be very profitable business. It is not farfetched to imagine the future purchase of a cable company by a large corporation whose primary interest in its new acquisition is its information banks of consumer preferences and buying habits. Could, or should, the legislature prohibit such internal information transfers?[29]

In Canada a trend towards larger MSOs has become evident in recent years. Rogers has acquired major systems in Toronto, London, Calgary, Vancouver and Victoria, but it remains an independent company. Maclean Hunter Cable Television, however, is already part of a large communications conglomerate known as Maclean Hunter Limited. The possibility that identifiable personal information could be centralized in the case of a large multiple-system operator or could be transferred from a local operator to its parent company presents considerable threats to consumer privacy. Rogers, for example, owns 50% of Cableshare Limited, a data processing company located in London, Ontario, which until recently handled the billing functions of Rogers cable subsidiaries. It is not clear to what extent this company centralized at least certain information about Rogers subscribers from across Canada.[30]

As part of its general regulation of the cable television and telephone industries, the CRTC controls the transfer of ownership of cable companies in Canada. In 1974 the CRTC denied as premature "the ownership of a cable undertaking by a company operating in the field of computer services. . . ." Current CRTC rules, which are under review, forbid the granting of "broadcasting receiving undertaking" licenses to companies in which banks hold substantial equity.[31] In part because the CRTC has not paid much attention to personal privacy issues to date, it is unlikely that concern for privacy will limit the growth of cable companies through consolidation, especially if difficult financial conditions continue.

INTERACTIVE SERVICES—REALITIES AND EXPECTATIONS

Experimentation with interactive cable has been in process since the 1970s, but two-way television has only become a reality in the last few years. Today, cable television companies, plagued by financial difficulties, regard interactive cable services as a major potential source of new revenue. Since the cable penetration rate in Canada is already rather high—reaching 81% of homes passed by cable in London, Ontario, 73% in Toronto and 88% in Vancouver—cable companies cannot grow simply by adding new subscribers.[32] Cable companies have therefore hoped that the variety of new specialized non-broadcast services would prove to be an additional attraction in selling basic cable service, and that they would improve the overall use of the existing cable plant. More importantly, the additional revenue generated from two-way services would help defray the costs involved in building and rebuilding cable systems.

These expectations have been especially true for Rogers Cablesystems and Telecable Videotron. The latter sees cable television as a way of delivering to consumers a full range of specialized services on a variety of channels. Telecable Videotron also regards new services as an added attraction in selling its basic product in the province of Quebec, where only 51.5% of households have access to cable versus 71.5% for Canada as a whole. At 1981 CRTC hearings in Vancouver Ed Jarmain, then chairman of the Cable Telecommunications Research Institute, explained that the traditional business of cable TV had leveled off, subscriber rates had not kept pace with inflation, much cable plant was old, inadequate and obsolete, and two-way capability had been almost non-existent, adding that "profitable new services are urgently needed now to bolster profits and justify the substantial new capital investments."[33] So far, however, Canadian cable companies are uncertain as to the profitability of interactive cable and question whether revenues to be garnered from it will offset the extensive capital costs necessary to make two-way services possible.

Although cable television has traditionally been much more advanced in Canada than in the United States, and despite the considerably lower penetration rate in the U.S., the pressure of competing for local cable television franchises has led to a much more extensive development of interactive cable services there. (In order to win an American franchise today a cable company must promise a variety of two-way services and a large number of channels. Many companies, however, are finding it hard to keep these promises, because of the heavy capital costs involved in cabling a community.) Yet even given the more advanced status of two-way services in the U.S., as of June 1984 only 350,000 U.S. households actually subscribed to interactive cable services. This represents a penetration level of only .4% of all TV homes and about 10% of all homes subscribing to cable.

Two-Way Services Currently Available

North American companies are at present offering interactive services for such purposes as banking, shopping, education, monitoring and surveillance, entertainment, information retrieval and message delivery. According to the National Cable Television Association, about 100 U.S. firms either offer two-way cable or have such systems in the works.[34] In Canada both Rogers and Videotron currently offer or have plans to offer two-way services.

The most well-known two-way commercial service in North America is the QUBE system introduced in Columbus, OH by Warner Amex Cable Communications Inc. in 1977. It serves approximately 30,000 homes in Columbus. The QUBE system has since been extended to Cincinnati, Pittsburgh,* Houston, Dallas, Milwaukee and the suburbs of St. Louis and Chicago. Warner Amex is the sixth largest U.S. MSO with 1.4 million basic subscribers to its cable systems.[35]

In Canada the most advanced cable company in terms of development of interactive two-way systems is Le Groupe Videotron, which has created a joint venture, Le Groupe Videoway Inc., with GTECH Corp. of Rhode Island and a Quebec government agency. After some delays its two-way services are expected to be fully interactive in May 1985. The integrated home information system known as Vidacom and/or Videoway will be able to handle two-way transactions for banking, electronic mail, teleshopping, opinion polling, alarm systems and information retrieval.[36] (See Chapter 4 for detailed descriptions of each of these services.)

Rogers Cablesystems Inc. has developed marketing and technical experience with interactive systems in both the U.S. and Canada. Its system in Portland, OR, started up in the fall of 1982, is said to be more advanced than QUBE. The Portland system offers pay-per-view services, channel monitoring and public opinion-polling; there are plans to introduce security services in the near future. The first two-way service available in the state of New York was the fire alarm system operated in Rogers' Syracuse franchise. Rogers is also in the process of developing interactive systems in Los Angeles and Minneapolis. Although Maclean Hunter has no interactive trials currently underway in Canada, it is developing such systems for its franchises in New Jersey and Michigan. All of the interactive services discussed in Chapter 4 have either been promised or put in place in one or another of the American franchises held by these two major Canadian MSOs.

Rogers Cablesystems has a number of experimental interactive services in place in Canada, but the pace of development has slowed, compared to some of its enthusiastic predictions of the early 1980s. Its 1983 *Annual Report* admits that "many early notions of a 'Wired City' were, and remain today, overly optimistic. Management's approach in this area is to emphasize practical two-way applications which are commercially viable in today's marketplace." Rogers' current emphasis is on alarm and security services and

---

*In the first quarter of 1984 TCI agreed to purchase the Pittsburgh, PA cable system from Warner Amex Cable Communications.

pay-per-view programming. Yet its perception of the future is based on the premise that "to effectively tap the consumer's discretionary entertainment dollar, systems must have maximum channel capacity, must be addressable and must have fully interactive capabilities."[37]

Videotex

Another medium that can supply such interactive services as banking, shopping and information retrieval is videotex, a two-way delivery system which uses a television set and a keypad terminal, coupled with either a telephone wire and/or coaxial cable.

The first commercial videotex service in the U.S. went into operation in the Miami area on October 30, 1983. The system operator, Viewdata Corp. of America, is owned by Knight-Ridder Newspapers, Inc., which plans to expand Viewtron, if successful, to other cities, such as Baltimore, Seattle, Boston and Philadelphia. This system is primarily used for information retrieval and delivers standard videotex graphics via special phone lines.[38]

Prior to Viewtron's start-up a number of U.S. companies were involved in videotex field trials in several American cities. In addition to Viewtron, a few other companies now offer videotex services and a major venture (Gateway) is slated for September 1984. Currently both CompuServe and Source Telecomputing Corp. offer computer-based videotex services, but neither system is capable of delivering color or sophisticated graphics.[39]

In March 1982 Infomart and Times Mirror Videotex Services of Los Angeles began a joint venture known as Videotex America to market and operate videotex systems in the U.S. The field trial—the Gateway experiment in 350 homes in southern California—provided transactional services using either telephone or cable communication systems. In September 1984 Gateway was first offered on a commercial basis in Southern California. Consumer services include teleshopping, telebanking and information retrieval.

Keycom's Keyfax Interactive Information Service, operated by Centel, Honeywell Corp. and Field Enterprises, is yet another videotex service which came on the market in 1984; this service is being offered in Chicago.

Despite the fact that existing U.S. videotex services have not been pulling in profits—Knight-Ridder projects a $17 million operating loss for Viewtron in 1984—this is an area in which a number of large corporations are expressing interest. Although no start-up date has yet been determined, IBM, CBS and Sears announced the formation of a joint videotex venture (Trintex) in February 1984 which will eventually deliver interactive services through telephone lines hooked up to personal computers.[40]

Telidon is the Canadian version of videotex. The federal government has spent a great deal of money to promote Telidon in recent years, yet the future of videotex remains uncertain.

In August 1983 there were 11 videotex field trials in operation in Canada; with some of these jointly operated, five were operated by cable companies and 11 by telephone companies. The latter had 1500 terminals, 75% of the total in the various experiments. Most of the trials emphasized information retrieval.

The first Canadian commercial Telidon service, known as Grassroots, began in May 1981 and serves farmers in Alberta, Saskatchewan, Manitoba and Ontario. It is a joint venture of the Manitoba telephone system and Infomart of Toronto. The system uses telephones and fiber optics to offer such services as information retrieval, home banking and teleshopping. One-half of the 2000 users are residential.[41]

In an evaluation report prepared for the federal government, Wescom Communications of Vancouver suggested the need to combine and unite technologies, such as cable and telephone systems, in order to promote Telidon. Wescom predicted that it would take five to 10 years for an acceptable level of return to be achieved for commercial ventures and Telidon programs and claimed that the development of such interactive services as teleshopping and telebanking is critical to the success of the commercial market.[42]

TECHNOLOGICAL REQUIREMENTS FOR TWO-WAY SERVICES

The technology currently exists for delivery of two-way services. Since almost all homes in North America have a television set, a primary component is already in place. Whether one uses a telephone wire or coaxial cable for transmission, the television set is the focal piece of equipment for the display of a wide range of new services.

Cable has better characteristics than telephone for the development and delivery of interactive services, such as the bandwidth required to handle multiple demands simultaneously and a high traffic or transmission capacity needed to accommodate the large volume of users of a delivery system. Broadband transmission refers to the ability of a coaxial cable to send several different signals down the same wire at the same time, all of them vibrating at different frequencies. Thus, one coaxial cable can carry a large number of channels.[43] A copper paired telephone wire can handle 24 voice channels. A coaxial cable can handle 35 channels on television or 21,000 voice channels, while fiber optics has 200 times the capacity of cable. The physical carrying capacity of cable is about 100,000 times the carrying capacity of a telephone line.[44] Telephone wires also have substantial deficiencies in the delivery of pictures as compared to cable.

The various technical advantages of cable over telephone systems are especially significant given the digital character of the proposed interactive systems. Up to now, radio, telephone and television have operated using the analog mode, in which data have continuously variable physical qualities. In the new digital mode data are broken down into discrete bits of information for transmission.[45] Since it is capable of digital communication without the need for a sophisticated converter at the receiving end, cable may be the ideal medium for the introduction of new interactive services.

At the same time, the current trend in communications technology is towards a convergence of modes, so that previously distinct systems—such as cable, telephone wires and computer lines—are becoming indistinguishable. South of San Francisco, for example, Pacific Telephone is planning to construct a 422-mile hybrid fiber-optic/coaxial cable network to provide full two-way service, including pay-per-view TV, videotex and computer messaging, to 50,000 households.[46]

Despite the technological advantages of cable, a number of technical problems need to be resolved before up-to-date operating cable systems are in place. In Canada, where some cable companies have a 30-year history, cable transmission systems are often very old. It is both difficult and expensive to rebuild the systems to handle new services. Even in the U.S., where the number of cable subscribers has grown to 33.7 million by mid-1984, a number of cable systems still have 12 channels or less—"reflecting the time it takes to upgrade systems built before recent technological innovations."[47]

Canadian cable companies are engaged in continuous rebuilding of their systems, especially now that pay television has been introduced. Rogers has long-term plans to make its entire physical plant capable of handling two-way services. Even though Maclean Hunter is not currently planning the introduction of any interactive systems in Canada, all of their new physical plant is two-way capable, as is true for all of their U.S. systems as well. In the province of Quebec, cable systems serving 50% of Telecable Videotron subscribers now have two-way capabilities.

The introduction of two-way services by cable companies also requires a much higher technical standard than the simple transmission of television signals along the system. Currently, thousands of trouble spots exist in any typical cable system as a television signal is carried either by underground cable wires or by cables attached to telephone or power company poles. Problems of noise or ingress are greatly increased when two-way amplifiers are used; more sophisticated systems of amplifiers are being developed. A number of other difficulties exist, but suffice it to say that making an interactive system operational requires high-level engineering skills as well as substantial capital outlays.

Addressability

The introduction of new cable services requires that the subscribing home be equipped with an addressable converter. This is a box attached to a television set which permits the cable or telephone company to release special programming or services to those customers requesting them. The company's headend computer is thus able to "address" particular contents to a particular subscriber. Pay television operates primarily through one-way addressable systems. In a two-way system, in addition to the cable operator's ability to control transmission to the viewer, the subscriber is able to transmit information to the cable company.

Most addressable converters are not yet two-way capable, but it is possible that they soon will be. For the moment, a subscriber often uses the telephone to order the specific service that will eventually be delivered in an addressable fashion over the cable. Once a cable company has made the commitment to the installation of addressable converters in particular homes, a major first step has been taken in the implementation of a two-way system.

The addressable units used by Rogers are made by Zenith in Canada while Nabu Manufacturing Corp. of Ottawa is working with Ottawa Cablevision on the development of two-way cable equipment. In general, manufacturers of equipment necessary for the introduction of two-way services are in a critical position to encourage and stimulate their use, especially by means of joint ventures, which can also help to reduce start-up costs.

THE OUTLOOK FOR INTERACTIVE SERVICES

Most plans for the introduction of two-way services in Canada and the U.S. have been at least delayed by the general economic difficulties of the early 1980s. In addition, as we have seen, there are a variety of technical problems in developing two-way services. There are also problems of finding a consumer market large enough to warrant the heavy capital expenditures made by cable and telephone companies and the suppliers of interactive services, such as banks and retailers. It seems evident that more joint ventures will develop between system operators, such as cable and/or telephone companies, and information providers/equipment suppliers, and that cable and telephone companies will lease channels to third parties to offer services.

Especially given the recent state of the economy, it is not difficult to locate skeptics and pessimists about the future of two-way services. Interactive services are very expensive to implement and not very profitable and, according to the manager of a local Canadian cable company, no one in Canada or the United States has made any money out of new cable services. He correctly notes that a number of cable companies that had plans to introduce new services by 1984 have now changed their minds. At a conference in Toronto on May 23, 1984, Eric Wimberley, a vice-president of the Canadian Cable Television Association, stated that "although a very few cable systems are experimenting with two-way services even now, in our opinion it will be some time before these services become widespread."

Not all cable industry participants and observers share this negative outlook. In various interviews and public statements, Gustave Hauser, former chairman of Warner Amex, has stated his belief that interactive services promise a great future for the cable industry. And audiences at meetings of the National Cable Television Association and the Direct Mail/Marketing Association in the spring of 1982 learned that "trends in American society are very favourable for marketing interactive home-to-market systems."[48] In a front-page story on the future of cable television on September 29, 1982 *The New York Times* concluded that, despite all of the sobering economic realities, "industry analysts still see cable as offering a cornucopia of programs and futuristic services, including movies, sports events and concerts on a pay-per-view basis, burglary and fire protection, banking transactions, newspapers and magazines."

A more sober assessment of the evolving situation appeared in *The New York Times* on March 28, 1984 under the title: "Two-Way Cable TV Falters." Focusing on cutbacks in QUBE programming because it has not proved profitable, the story indicated that for the foreseeable future the two-way service would be used primarily for such lucrative features as pay-per-view films, which subscribers can order on impulse.

In an opening statement in the Rogers *1982 Annual Report,* published early in 1983, Ted Rogers emphasized that "the era of in-home electronic communications is just beginning." In his view, "cable technology provides an efficient multi-channel broadband system which has no competitive equal for delivering entertainment, information and educational services to the home." He emphasized that in the future, Rogers "will operate increasingly as a marketing company, retailing an expanding variety of...products."

As noted earlier in this chapter, Rogers Cablesystems had reduced its level of expectations for interactive services by the beginning of 1984 and is emphasizing certain practical applications. Its arch-rival in Canada, Maclean Hunter Cable, is even more pessimistic at present: "We have no plans at the moment to enter into any form of two-way interactive cable. Certainly the technology exists, and we are equipped to provide it. But again, it's an existing technology looking for a non-existent market. The time is not yet right."[49]

David Carlisle, former president of Infomart, has remained one of the most visibly optimistic North American proponents of two-way services. He expects that two-way television as a transaction medium for banking, shopping and information retrieval will achieve a 30% to 40% penetration of Canadian homes by the end of the 1980s. Since Infomart is a leading North American company in the videotex field, Carlisle's visionary optimism is not surprising. But it is symptomatic of the uncertain future of two-way services that Carlisle and Infomart parted company in the summer of 1983. According to press reports, Carlisle believes Infomart was doing too little to push video-tex "into a mass consumer technology for the home," especially in comparison with fast-paced American videotex developments. By contrast, his immediate successor, William G. Hutchison, expected videotex to be in use in only 5% to 7% of Canadian households by the end of the decade.[50]

Other observers continue to suggest that the Canadian experience with Telidon and the British experience with Prestel indicate that there is not yet any significant home consumer market for interactive services. Prestel has obtained almost no residential users for its information retrieval services. *The Economist* noted that this videotex system will have to await the introduction of two-way cable before it will really catch on in the home.[51]

In light of their economic difficulties, cable companies in the U.S. and Canada do not have any incentives to offer interactive services until they become commercially viable, except perhaps to use these as a selling point to promote cable penetration or to win franchises. One of the leading multiple system operators in Canada, for example, will not enter into any type of new cable service that does not pay its own way. The experiments described in Chapter 4 are attempts to demonstrate the technical feasibility of two-way systems and the existence of a consumer market for interactive services.

A number of cable industry participants believe that the future of two-way cable will involve the careful introduction of a mix of programming and non-programming services. The argument is that such a mix is essential, since neither will be self-supporting, and the cost of installing the appropriate hardware in a home will have to be met somehow. Thus cable companies are devoting considerable attention to the development of programming and especially non-programming services on an operating-business basis, if possible. The introduction of non-programming services in particular is generally risky and expensive, especially since consumer interest is not yet very strong. Indeed, it is difficult for the cable companies to assess just what services consumers will be willing to purchase. The executives responsible for the management of cable companies are thus in a position to have to determine which of the various types of interactive services are most likely to meet with success in terms of consumer acceptance.

One clue may be found in responses made by consumers polled by the London Privacy Survey conducted in the late fall of 1982. While about 54% of respondents said that they would use two-way cable services, the percentage very interested or interested in various types of services was as follows: security services, 80%; information retrieval, 54%; telebanking, 52%; tele-education, 50%; pay-per-view services, 42%; and teleshopping, 34%.[52]

It is clear that controversy exists as to the viability of interactive services and that, among those who forecast future success for two-way systems, there is a varying level of expectation as to how soon these systems and services will become widespread. Based on a review of the available literature and interviews with persons in the industry, this volume concludes that there is no doubt about the long-term future of the "electronic cottage"; the only questions that remain are what medium will win the race to deliver home information and communication services—i.e., coaxial cable, telephone wires, satellite transmission, fiber optics, or combinations of any of these—and how long the process will take.

In whatever way these questions resolve themselves, it is vital that both business and government take steps to ensure the protection of personal privacy in the use of interactive systems. The preconditions for protecting privacy should be established now, even if industry is not fully certain what the future will bring.

NOTES

1. *The Home Video & Cable Report* (Knowledge Industry Publications, Inc.), various issues; *Cable Advertising Merchandising and Programming Report* (*CAMP*) (Knowledge Industry Publications, Inc.), July 9, 1984. (Hereafter cited as *CAMP*.)

2. *Cable Communications Magazine*, XLIX (November 1983), pp. 26–27.

3. Based on statistics in *CAMP*, July 9, 1984.

4. *Ibid*. Subscription figures are as of January 1, 1984.

5. See *Tele-Communications, Inc. 1983 Annual Report* (Denver, CO, 1984).

6. *CAMP*, July 9, 1984. Subscription figures are as of January 1, 1984.

7. See Time Incorporated, *1983 Annual Report* (New York, NY, 1984).

8. *CAMP*, July 9, 1984.

9. See *Westinghouse Electric Corp. 1983 Annual Report* (Pittsburgh, PA, 1984).

10. *CAMP*, July 9, 1984.

11. See Cox Communications, *1983 Annual Report* (Atlanta, GA, 1984).

12. *CAMP*, July 9, 1984.

13. See Storer Communications, Inc., *Annual Report*, 1983 (Miami, FL, 1984).

14. *CAMP*, July 9, 1984. Subscription figures are as of May 1, 1984.

15. See American Express Company, *Annual Report 1983* (New York, NY, 1984); and *Warner Communications Inc. 1983 Annual Report* (New York, NY, 1984).

16. *Cable Communications Magazine*, XLIX (November 1983), pp. 37–41, 48–49.

17. Details from *Cable Communications Magazine*, XLIX (November 1983), pp. 27, 41, 43, 45; and Rogers Cablesystems Inc., *1983 Annual Report* (Toronto, 1984).

18. *The Globe and Mail*, July 17, 1984, p. B9; and Rogers Cablesystems Inc., *1983 Annual Report.*

19. See Hawley L. Black, "Telecable Videotron's 'Vidacom': A Progress Report," *Cable Communications Magazine*, XLVIII, No. 8 (August 1982), pp. 12–15; Pierre Sormany, "La television du FUTUR," *L'Actualite*, VIII (March 1983), pp. 27–33; and *Cable Communications Magazine*, XLIX (November 1983), pp. 37, 41, 45.

20. See *Maclean Hunter 1983 Annual Report* (Toronto, 1984); and *Cable Communications Magazine*, XLIX (November 1983), p. 45.

21. *Cable Communications Magazine*, XLIX (November 1983), pp. 43, 45.

22. See Canadian Cable Television Association, *The 1980's Challenge: New Consumer Services Through Cable Television.* Special Report. Plenary IV, CCTA Annual Convention, Vancouver, May 1980. (Ottawa: Canadian Cable Television Association, 1980), pp. 1–12. (Hereafter cited as CCTA, *The 1980's Challenge.*)

23. See the informed treatment of the history of the introduction of pay TV and the advance predictions in R. Brian Woodrow and Kenneth B. Woodside, eds., *The Introduction of Pay-TV in Canada. Issues and Implications* (Montreal: The Institute for Research on Public Policy, 1982), pp. xxi, 8, 31–56, 133. Reviews of the first year can be found in *The Financial Post*, December 31, 1983, p. 5; *The Globe and Mail*, January 7, 1984, p. 10; and *The Globe and Mail*, January 10, 1984, p. B11; see also *The Globe and Mail*, July 28, 1984, p. B7.

24. *The New York Times*, November 24, 1983, pp. A1, C22.

25. *The Economist*, 282 (March 5, 1982), p. 25. North American telephone companies already use fiber optics in trunk routes.

26. CCTA, *The 1980's Challenge*, pp. 6–7.

27. *Washington Post,* July 28, 1984, p. B1.

28. See Deanna Collingwood Nash and John B. Smith, *Interactive Home Media and Privacy.* Prepared for the Office of Policy Planning, U.S. Federal Trade Commission (Washington, DC: Collingwood Associates, Inc., January 1981), p. 11; Robert Ellis Smith, "One Perspective on Warner Amex Cable," *Privacy Journal,* IX (February 1983), pp. 3–6.

29. Testimony of Norma Rollins, "The Future of Cable Television in New York State," New York State Assembly's Standing Committee on Governmental Operations, April 22, 1982, p. 3.

30. Charles Dalfen, *An Industry in Transition. Regulatory Aspects of the New Technology.* Royal Commission on Newspapers Research Reports, April 6, 1981, p. 102; Cableshare Inc., *Annual Report 1982* (London, Ontario, 1982), p. 10; Rogers Cablesystems Inc., *1982 Annual Report* (Toronto, 1983), p. 12.

31. Dalfen, *Industry in Transition,* p. 71, 102.

32. Canadian Radio-television and Telecommunications Commission, *Facts Digest* (January 1982), pp. 6, 7.

33. Canadian Radio-television and Telecommunications Commission, "Public Hearings on Non-programming Services," Toronto, March 10–12, 1981, pp. 216, 258–259. (Hereafter cited as CRTC, *Hearings.*) See also CRTC, *Hearings,* Vancouver, April 28–30, 1981, p. 294.

34. *Privacy Times,* II, No. 1 (January 19, 1982), p. 3.

35. QUBE is described in detail in John Wicklein, *Electronic Nightmare: The New Communications and Freedom* (New York: The Viking Press, 1979), Chapter 2; Nash and Smith, *Interactive Home Media and Privacy,* pp. 33–57.

36. See the descriptions of Vidacom in *Cable Communications Magazine,* XLVIII, No. 8 (August 1982), pp. 12–15; and Dept. of Communications, *Telidon Trials and Services* (Ottawa: Dept. of Communications, 1983), pp. 77–78.

37. Rogers Cablesystems Inc., *1983 Annual Report,* pp. 9, 29.

38. *Computerworld,* November 14, 1983, p. 2.

39. *The Home Video & Cable Report,* February 20, 1984, April 23, 1984 and June 11, 1984.

40. *Ibid.*

41. Dept. of Communications, *Telidon Trials and Services,* pp. 41–43, 97.

42. This paragraph is based on Peter J. Booth and Russel M. Wills, *Telidon Evaluation Executive Summary Report. Major Policy Issues and Recommendations* (Wescom Communications and Research Studies, Vancouver, B.C., August 1983, Mimeographed), pp. 23, 24, 30, 32, 36, 43, 44 and 52.

43. Francis Spiller Associates, *New Broadcasting and Communications Services* (*A Perspective*) (Nepean, Ontario: Francis Spiller Associates, September 1980), p. 14. (Hereafter cited as Spiller, *New Broadcasting and Communications Services.*) See also CRTC, *Hearings,* Toronto, March 10–12, 1981, p. 254.

44. Spiller, *New Broadcasting and Communications Services,* p. 7; Dalfen, *Industry in Transition,* p. 22.

45. Spiller, *New Broadcasting and Communications Services,* p. 4. Spiller states that "it is already possible to digitise television signals, and telephone companies are already converting voice traffic to a digital form." (Private communication, February 28, 1983.)

46. See the discussion of convergence in *The New Republic,* October 3, 1983, p. 33. Pacific Telephone's plans are discussed in Cable Telecommunications Research Institute, *Interaction,* IV (December 1983), p. 5.

47. *The New York Times,* September 28, 1982, pp. 1, C22. The figure of about 5 million cable subscribers in Canada furnishes some sense of the huge market for cable television in the U.S. See also *Cable Communications Magazine,* XLIX (November 1983).

48. See the report in *Privacy Journal,* VIII, No. 7 (May 1982), p. 6.

49. *Maclean Hunter 1983 Annual Report* (Toronto, 1984), p. 4.

50. Martin Dewey, "Two-way Television Brings Fresh Outlook to World," *The Globe and Mail,* March 29, 1982, p. R20; Jonathan Chevreau, "Videotex Visionary Leaves Top Infomart Position," *The Globe and Mail,* August 6, 1983, p. B4. Carlisle is now president of Carlisle Videotex Consultants Inc.

51. See Jonathan Chevreau, "Canada is Still Awaiting Videotex Take-off," *The Globe and Mail,* June 26, 1982, p. B1; *The Economist,* 282, No. 7227 (March 6, 1982), p. 27.

52. Neil J. Vidmar, "Privacy and Two-Way Cable Television: A Study of Canadian Public Opinion," (Downsview, Ontario: Ontario Ministry of Transportation and Communications, May 1983), pp. 39, 41, 43, 51.

4

Interactive Services and Their Implications for Personal Privacy

THE TECHNOLOGY OF INTERACTIVE SERVICES

Although some cable companies in the United States currently use the telephone for the upstream part of an interactive service,* the introduction of a true two-way cable service requires a system similar to Warner Amex's QUBE operation in Columbus, Ohio, and various other American cities. This essentially involves the installation of an addressable converter that can communicate on a two-way basis with a television set in the home via coaxial cable. QUBE is available in Chicago, Cincinnati, Columbus, Dallas, Houston, Pittsburgh and St. Louis.

QUBE

Since the architecture of the computers has a lot to do with the storage and transmission of personal information in a two-way system, it is useful to describe the QUBE system as it existed in Columbus in January 1981. The system then had three computers at the headend, one used for polling, one used as a studio computer (the first two being linked), and one used for billing and administrative services. The link between the first two and third computers required the transfer of magnetic tapes.[1] The polling computer at the headend checked the on-off status of the television set, the channel being viewed, the last response button pushed, if a response poll was underway and security system alerts. The polling computer transferred individual data to the

---

*Data which travel upstream in an interactive system is that information which originates in the subscribing household and is transmitted to the cable company's headend computer. Downstream refers to material originating at the cable company which is transmitted to the subscribing household.

studio computer to prepare statistical data on viewer selections and records of individual use of premium channels for billing purposes. The third computer matched address codes of users to the names and addresses of individuals, who then received itemized bills for pay-per-view services on a monthly basis. Individual billing records were kept nine months for routine business purposes, and summary data were kept indefinitely.

Collingwood Associates noted in its valuable review of QUBE computers that "the three-computer configuration offers the obvious advantage for security and privacy purposes of separating the polling function, where individual activity is recorded and accumulated, from the billing function, where user codes and accompanying data are linked with actual names and addresses."[2] In fact, QUBE plans to use a single computer in the future, which would end the physical separation among the three computers, and would add logical or software security precautions. At present QUBE in Columbus uses two computers.

At the headend of any two-way system, including QUBE in Columbus, the central computers sweep each outlet in the cable system every 10 seconds for various types of signals from a subscriber. They can produce readouts in either hard copy or on video display terminals. The central system also records all of the information coming and going from the central station on voice recorder (for insurance purposes), which is manned 24 hours a day, seven days a week.

Use of Computers in Interactive Systems

While QUBE can be seen as the forerunner of all interactive systems, others have recently started up and a number are in the planning stages. All interactive services, however, depend on the extensive use of computers. At the time of the CRTC (Canadian Radio-television and Telecommunications Commission) non-programming hearings in the spring of 1981 (in both Toronto and Vancouver) Rogers' so-called "Wonderbox" had not yet been developed; this referred to the keypad that would be used in the home. Rogers then owned a total of nine computers in London, Ontario, Calgary and Toronto which were used for maintaining subscriber billing systems, but indicated that it would probably need new types of computers to handle interactive services.[3] Rogers has built a "Super System" for the management of subscriber information, which is designed to accommodate addressable and interactive services: "It has been designed on a modular basis so that as they become available, new services can be controlled through the same system."[4] This system is now on-stream in all Canadian outlets and is being introduced in stages in U.S. franchises. As noted earlier, Rogers now has two regional data centers in Toronto and Vancouver.

In London and Brampton, Ontario, Rogers Cable TV wants information for each city's computerized traffic control system to be carried over a cable network, rather than via telephone lines. According to Gordon Symonds, the London general manager, "the installation of the two-way system needed for the computer system would give a good base for future expansion of the two-way interactive service to home subscribers."[5] The London example illustrates the very significant point that once a cable company has installed computers and addressable converters with two-way capacity, there are no limitations on the introduction of as many interactive services as can be cost-justified by sales to consumers.

The actual configuration of computers and two-way services adopted by a local cable company or the MSO that owns it will have a great deal to do with the amount of personal information that is ultimately stored in the headend computers. For certain services, the headend computers only act as a gateway to the machines of specific service suppliers, such as retailers, banks or information providers. On the other hand, certain interactive services produce data that are stored only momentarily in the cable company's headend computer, such as those used for channel monitoring. Although it is possible to program a headend computer so that no personal information is stored, this would preclude such essential commercial activities as the preparation of itemized bills for individual subscribers. But a computer is not capable of any further information manipulations, unless individual data are stored in an accessible place within the system. Thus, in certain situations, non-storage of data is a crucial protection for personal privacy.

At the CRTC's non-programming hearings in Vancouver in April 1981 the Alarm Association of British Columbia argued that its security companies could better protect privacy than cable operators: "For one thing, the assembling of the data would be decentralized, rather than it all funnelling into a central computer controlled by a single entity, and the signals will be diversified into the hands of a number of people." The latter situation would be true, of course, if the cable company's central computers were being used solely in a transactional mode to transmit individual records to banks or retailers. In such circumstances, the headend computer would simply verify the customer's identity, but this might also require the storage of verification data. Since some systems now in the planning stages can handle 1000 transactions per second, it might not be practical to store the voluminous amounts of information generated by such a large number of transactions. On the other hand, continued developments in storage capacity mean that it has become increasingly cheap to store large amounts of data.

A difference of opinion sometimes still exists about the importance of inexpensive record storage to the privacy interests of individuals. In cable privacy hearings before the New York State Legislature in May 1982, Attorney General Robert Abrams claimed that it was easier to store data than to purge or erase them. Others have pointed out the cost of including purging routines in software. In actual fact, the costs of the central processing unit and primary memory in large computers have been reduced even more than has the cost of storage. Stored records can be erased by simple reuse of the tapes, a procedure used by Bell Canada with its individual long-distance billing records after a six-month period. Moreover, purge routines can be run at off-hours, when computer time is much cheaper; freeing up disc or tape capacity is also a significant benefit of erasure for computer users. Finally, it is easy and not that costly to design a set of very simple and automatic purge routines for stored personal data, which can be of significant benefit to the privacy of individuals.[6]

Software Design

In terms of concerns for subscriber privacy, the software in the headend computers is obviously a very vulnerable part of any interactive system. Since the programs for specific services tend to be written by modules, one could conceivably build into each module appropriate protections for the confidentiality of personal information. In an interactive opinion-polling system, such as the one used by Rogers in Portland, OR, no individual personal records or opinions are stored, even though it is possible to do so. It is thus important that, insofar as possible, the software for any one of these services should be designed so as to make it impossible for identifiable individual information to be stored and subsequently retrieved. The software for opinion-polling, for example, can be designed in such a way as to make it impossible for anyone to know how an individual person or household voted on a particular issue; as results flow into the headend computer they would simply be tabulated and then obliterated. It is not necessary to separate the software for opinion-polling from the software for a tele-education course. One software routine can have a separate flag for collecting data from opinion-polling and include an automatic purge routine for destroying the data on specific students after a stipulated period that covered the end of the course in question.[7] The Portland system does not record individual course responses because of existing concerns about privacy.

Since in an interactive information retrieval system a request from a particular household can be temporarily registered, it might be possible to produce a profile of all the information a given subscriber requested over a certain period of time. Companies might also have to record the specific pages used by an individual subscriber in order to determine the fee to be charged for information in a data base that is subject to royalties. This is a good illustration of how complying with a particular requirement (in this case, determining proper royalty payments) further increases the potential for invasion of personal privacy, although an automatic purge routine designed to operate 90 days, for example, after a record was created would reduce the risk. An alternative approach is that charges could be monitored for purposes of copyright payment without recording the actual names of individuals obtaining access to data. Or, if charges were based on time used on the system, there would be no real need to record the information retrieved by a particular subscriber.

Another reason why cable companies record certain types of personal information is to guard against disputes over billing for particular services. The company that originally offered pay-per-view in Columbus, OH encountered problems with claims that no one in the family had watched a particular program. In Portland, Rogers subscribers have to use a particular request code on the keypad in their home in order to obtain a specific service.

On the whole, companies offering interactive services have to give much more thought than they have done up to now to the privacy implications of the storage and transmission of personal information to and through their central computers. This may be as simple an act of consciousness-raising as instructing the designers of software for two-way systems to keep the storage of data on individuals to an absolute minimum and then to purge all stored data at built-in intervals. A good model can be found in the practices employed by the Intelpost facsimile mail service between Washington, DC and London, England. Once transmitted, a message can be "wiped off the memories of the computers at either end."[8] Such a technological solution could be very important for such interactive services as public opinion-polling and information retrieval.

PAY-PER-VIEW SERVICES

Pay-per-view systems are the most attractive of the proposed interactive services, although their proliferation will no doubt depend on the degree of market penetration achieved by pay cable itself. The installation of two-way addressable converters in individual homes could easily speed the introduction of pay television on a pay-per-view basis. (With pay-per-view the viewer pays for a particular event he wants to watch.) Production and cable companies are anxious to reap a large financial return from specific pay-per-view events, such as a boxing match, a movie or a concert. Significant pay-per-view events include the June 1982 Holmes/Cooney boxing match, the February 1983 showing of *The Pirates of Penzance* (simultaneous with theatrical release of the film) and a live concert by The Who in Toronto.

Some of the interactive systems in the United States use the telephone instead of cable as the means by which an individual can order a particular pay-per-view event. The same system can also be used for security services, teleshopping, opinion-polling, education and information retrieval. The two-way Portland cable system owned by Rogers, which became operative in the fall of 1982, enables subscribers to order individual programs by entering a specific two-digit event request code on their home keypad. Individual data are stored for the purpose of preparing an itemized bill that lists exactly which programs the household in question has viewed. Rogers also makes pay-per-view available in its Minneapolis, MN and Southern California cable systems.[9]

Pay-per-view television has evidently enjoyed a positive reception in Portland, which has a population of about 1 million. On average, one out of five subscribers tunes in to a U.S. $5 pay-per-event program each month. In order to obtain particular pay services before the fall of 1982, subscribers had to use the telephone to furnish their name, address and the number of their converter. According to Rogers, no subscriber has raised any questions about privacy in this system. Telecable Videotron in Montreal has for a number of years operated a similar on-demand service using phone lines. A subscriber can order any one of 5000 programs available to all users but which are scheduled at the request of the individual subscriber.[10]

In the U.S. at least 500,000 households have cable equipment enabling pay-per-view individual program selection, a number which is expected to swell rapidly. Gustave Hauser, former president of Warner Amex, believes that there could be as many as 20 million such homes by 1987. Paul Kagan, a leading industry analyst, thinks that pay-per-view cable is capable of yielding $2 billion in annual revenues by 1990. For the June 1982 Holmes/Cooney heavyweight boxing match, 40% of the available pay-per-view audience paid $15 apiece to view the fight. Pay-per-view is expected to provide subscribers with major sporting events, individual films, theatrical productions and concerts, although some scepticism continues to be expressed about its prospects for financial success.[11]

A June 1983 Yankee Group report on new services for cable and telephone companies regarded pay-per-view as the most lucrative and obvious service for joint provision by the two types of delivery systems. The Yankee Group estimated that by the end of 1985 21% of U.S. cable subscribers (now totaling more than 32 million households) will have access to pay-per-view programming, which will justify the investment required to produce, promote and distribute pay-per-view events. The research group also singled out the advantages of the hybrid delivery system being developed in Canada by the Cable Telecommunications Research Institute in cooperation with Bell Canada and Rogers Cablesystems, since it requires only a telephone and a one-way addressable converter in the home.[12]

Canadian cable industry observers anticipate the introduction in the next several years of pay-per-view services using at least one-way cable technology. The factors hindering speedier progress are the preoccupation with the introduction of pay television itself, the state of the economy, cultural concerns and the cost of upgrading facilities so that two-way cable can be introduced.

In a one-way system a telephone will be used to pre-order a particular pay-per-view service. Cable companies favor pay-per-view via a fully interactive two-way system because of viewer propensity toward impulse buying. In the Rogers Portland system, for example, pay-per-view trials have demonstrated that as many as 50% of the orders for a given program are placed two hours before it airs.

With any type of pay-per-view system the cable companies know specifically which programs a household is watching. The system offered in Toronto hotels by a Rogers subsidiary, Transworld Communications, uses the telephone for pay-per-view and permits the service provider to know what movies have been watched in specific hotel rooms. Knowing that a particular household or hotel room has watched a movie such as *Gone With the Wind* is normally an innocuous piece of information, except that the viewing of certain types of pay-per-view services (and X-rated movies already available in hotel rooms) might be more sensitive information, especially if combined with other subscriber data. For example, in the 100-channel environment of the future, there might be separate channels for adult films, feminists, homosexuals, fundamentalists, right-wing groups or radicals. Some persons might want to conceal their viewing of a particular channel. According to *The London Free Press* (December 4, 1982 issue) several U.S. satellite services already received in Canada include such channels as the following: Escapade/Playboy, Eros (erotic films), Praise the Lord, Christian Broadcasting Network, National Jewish Television and National Spanish Television Network.

It is the responsibility of the cable industry to keep pay-per-view information confidential and store it only as long as necessary. The QUBE subscriber agreement in Columbus provides that the "subscriber's 'premium' channel program selections will be recorded on a computer printout. Such records shall be kept strictly confidential except for purposes of serving subscriber's account. No other individualized records will be developed of either viewing selections or interactive responses unless the subscriber has been advised in advance and given adequate opportunity not to participate."[13] Although there is not yet any legal way for such an agreement to be enforced, a subscriber can discontinue service at any time and perhaps sue the cable company for breach of contract if confidentiality is violated.

Another privacy-related problem arises when a subscriber phones the cable company to question a pay-per-view bill for a particular month. Since the appropriate data are stored at least temporarily, a third person could attempt to learn the viewing habits of a particular individual, and the telephone operators would need a way of authenticating the caller's identity.

An episode which occurred in Columbus, OH indicates that the possibility of obtaining access to the records of individuals watching pay-per-view events is not totally hypothetical. A local theater owner, who was prosecuted on obscenity charges for screening an allegedly pornographic film, learned that an abridged version of the same film had been offered on QUBE. The defense lawyer subpoenaed QUBE records in order to obtain identifiable information on local viewers who had ordered the film. The presiding judge, however, ordered the QUBE management to produce only the number of viewers who had ordered the film. Although Warner Amex has stated that the ruling would have been appealed to higher courts had it required further data disclosure, Alan Westin points out that "local judges could well rule differently in other cases, and the appellate courts might sustain those rulings where there is no statutory protection for the identified records."[14] There is a similar lack of protection for such records in Canada.

Some observers have suggested that the "undesired reception of objectionable or unwanted programming material" could be construed as a privacy issue. In my opinion, it is stretching the point to argue that this is a matter of privacy, since the subscriber can turn off the set, not subscribe to a particular pay-per-view event or lock out certain adult channels. In QUBE and other two-way systems that are currently being designed, terminal gates at either the headend or in the home can be activated to block the reception of unsuitable material for those who do not wish to receive it. The home can also be provided with a key-lock on the channel control.[15]

CHANNEL MONITORING

A capacity for channel monitoring is a frequent by-product of the installation of an interactive system; such capability exists in the Rogers public opinion-polling systems in London and Portland. Depending on the configuration adopted, the cable company's headend computer can scan and monitor TV usage in homes at intervals of six to 10 seconds. The system can tell whether the television set is in use, what channel is being watched and for how long.

Channel monitoring can occur 24 hours a day, seven days a week. This stands in contrast to the type of telephone service monitoring the Bell Canada staff conducts, which is kept to a minimum and is used only for brief periods when necessary. Circuits are tested only to determine whether they are in use before disconnecting them or when operators verify that a call has been completed. Sometimes monitoring is also undertaken on a random basis to develop measurement statistics for quality control, but the kinds of data collected are impersonal, such as the speed of operator answer or transmission quality.[16]

The kind of personal information that can be collected by means of channel monitoring has enormous attractions for companies involved in marketing. According to the president of a Toronto area cable company, "the ability to determine which households are watching which television channel at any given time is extremely important. Present survey techniques are either very approximate and therefore unreliable or are extremely expensive. Advertisers have a very major interest in knowing which programs, and if possible, which commercials are being watched. The programmers themselves would very much like accurate measurements of their audience...."[17] John Wicklein has written that "computerized two-way systems can make Nielsen and Arbitron ratings obsolete. No 'sampling' guesswork—the QUBE computer knew, down to the last household, how many sets were tuned to one of its channels. 'We can give the advertiser demographics we never had before—how many people in the $20,000–$30,000 bracket are watching this commercial, that sort of thing,' said a marketing executive."[18] Robert Ellis Smith has suggested that the risks of the QUBE system "appear not in actual abuses of subscriber information, but in the nature of the direct marketing activities of the widespread QUBE corporate family." He argues that the real value of the system to both Warner Communications and American Express "is as a producer of highly detailed and computerized marketing information about each of the families who subscribe to QUBE." Warner Cable's vice president of marketing boasted in May 1980 that QUBE is the ultimate vehicle for test marketing: "We know exactly who is watching, what they are watching, and when they are watching."[19]

Canadian cable companies are also discussing the prospects of having valuable personal information to market. It may become an important source of revenue for them, if purchasers can be persuaded to pay enough to help recover the substantial capital-intensive costs of the cable industry.

Sales and marketing persons for cable companies will have a strong incentive to generate more revenue by selling personal information in either aggregated or individual form to marketing firms. Norma Rollins of the New York Civil Liberties Union's Privacy Project testified before the New York State Assembly's Standing Committee on Governmental Operations in April 1982 that "the cable companies intend to use the information they collect to determine what other types of services to set up and market. Part of their internal mission, in fact, is to collect information which will give direction for future marketing." Since one of the key concerns in the industry in recent years has been audience fragmentation, cable companies will want to use data collected via two-way systems for demographic research on which viewers constitute the market for a particular channel.

Aggregate vs. Individual Data Gathering

From the point of view of personal privacy, it obviously makes a great difference whether the personal information collected by cable companies is used in aggregated or identifiable individual form. The general response of cable companies in the U.S. and Canada is that information on individuals will only be collected and used in aggregated form.[20] The Warner Amex privacy code (see Appendix) includes the following model principle:

> Warner Amex may develop bulk (non-individual) data concerning subscriber services for use in developing new services or improving existing services. Warner Amex will not make such bulk data available to third parties—whether affiliated or non-affiliated with Warner Amex—without first ensuring that the identity of individuals is not ascertainable from the data provided.

While this goal is laudable, it is not so easy to ensure the anonymity of individual data, and there are no assurances that all cable companies will follow the strict rules set forth by Warner Amex, especially in the face of importuning pressures from direct mail marketers. A spokesman for New York Attorney General Robert Abrams noted that cable firms suffered great financial losses in the start-up phase, because of the expensive promises made in franchising competitions: "The re-sale of the information they collect on subscribers is a very important source of revenue for new firms as they try to recoup their losses."[21]

The real pressure for access to data on individual subscribers will come from marketing firms. An episode reported in *The Wall Street Journal* on September 25, 1981 is illustrative of at least one extreme in market research technology. In a number of experimental tests conducted in various states, "market-research firms monitor and catalog the grocery store purchases of thousands of families and simultaneously transmit custom-tailored commercials to the same people via cable TV. Thus the power of the pitch can be measured on an individual basis."

For the last five years Information Resources Inc. of Chicago has been offering a service called Behaviorscan in Pittsfield, MA, Visalia, CA, Rome, GA, Grand Junction, CO and Williamsport, PA. Supermarket cash registers produce online reports of purchases by identifiable consumers, who receive either regular or specialized commercials over their cable TV screens through a device attached to the set. In this marketing research method, the company insists on informed consent from consumers, stores only aggregated information, and segregates the panelists's identities from the raw data. Nevertheless, the refusal rate for those asked to participate is 30%.[22] Although one might question the judgment of individual participants in such tests and services, the voluntary nature of the activity means that they cannot accuse the marketers of invading their privacy during the collection of primary data.

The moral of these experiments and services is that once channel monitoring begins to collect and store a great deal of personal information about the habits of consumers on a regular basis, the marketing industry is going to dream up more ways to use such personal data.

It will be difficult for companies offering interactive services to resist the financial pressure exerted to persuade them to allow access to individual data in identifiable or aggregated form, although they claim only to be interested in disseminating aggregated or statistical information. At one level one can agree with the comment by Collingwood Associates that "aggregation of the [individual] information, where each individual is not—and cannot be—identified, does not seem to raise a major privacy issue."[23] However, the risks of identifying specific individuals from a limited local area are significant, even when personal information has been aggregated for statistical purposes or when individual data have been made anonymous. There is a significant body of literature produced by statisticians on this particular point.

The collection of aggregated or statistical information also raises some important questions about group privacy. Marketers have a particular interest in linking aggregated information, derived from a source such as channel monitoring, with census tract data already available on a particular neighborhood, street or locality. Thus, the cable company can make available, even in aggregated form, statistics about what percentage of subscribers in a specific neighborhood watch particular programs or channels. Some individuals residing in a given neighborhood may not want statistics to be made available which indicate that 80% of the group watch a particular channel or program at least once a week, since such information may appear to reveal the group's political, sexual or religious preferences.

Concerning the problems associated with both the use of aggregated information and group privacy, it is useful to consider a statement made by Edmund Rapaport of Statistics Sweden:

> On occasions, statistical agencies have justified the right to utilization of [personal] data by maintaining that statistics are innocuous to the individual, as they report aggregated situations or conditions characterized by variables, to the exclusion of situations related to identifiable individuals. It is now frequently admitted that this argument will not hold water. Granted that there is some truth in the proposition that individuals cannot be directly identified from statistical reports, although in some cases the risk of disclosure is present. But statistics are not, and should not be, "harmless" in general terms. For example, statistics used in a social context can affect the situation of individual groups for better or for worse. Given this, the situation of the individual on whom information is included in administrative records can, on occasion, suffer detriment.[24]

Although a cable company may state that it has no real interest in the subscriber as an individual, except for billing purposes, channel monitoring may alienate privacy-conscious subscribers. While the software enabling channel monitoring may not always store individual information, a provision for such storage could easily be added on. Unfortunately for the subscriber, channel monitoring is normally an integral part of any two-way system, but the positive benefits (especially the goal of ensuring the proper operating performance of the home terminal) are offset by the risk the consumer takes of forfeiting some of his or her privacy.

Software used for channel monitoring should be designed to ensure that data on individual viewing habits be aggregated and then erased, with any kind of storage made impossible. Some companies are inclined to resist channel monitoring altogether, by not building that capability into the technical system. If a customer remains concerned about channel monitoring, individual subscriber data can even be removed from the aggregated data. A 1974 proposal from the government of Manitoba, studying the prospects for interactive services, argued "that subscribers should be able to disconnect their sets from program monitoring or polling-by-station, by simply throwing a switch attached to the home terminal. Some have suggested that a light or bell should be incorporated into any home terminal to warn a subscriber that a set is being monitored."[25] Such idiosyncratic prescriptions could proliferate, if cable companies do not self-regulate in advance.

SECURITY SERVICES

The furnishing of security services to individual households is one of the most popular current and proposed interactive cable services. A security system uses two-way cable or a telephone link to permit sensing devices to survey the status of each home continuously. By means of a direct link to the company offering the service, monitors alert fire or police departments or medical personnel in the event of smoke, a fire, a break-in or an illness. The operator, alerted by a sensor, telephones the home to verify the situation; if the phone is not answered, or the respondent fails to use a secret password, the authorities are alerted. A medical alert device, which is usually an addition to the standard surveillance and security services, can be activated by the user within several hundred feet of a household. The medical alert emergency alarm notifies the central station of the provider of the service (the service provider can be a cable, telephone or security company or an alliance of these), which keeps on file details concerning the needs of the subscriber, including blood type, allergies and reactions to drugs.

The New York Times reported in fall 1982 that "of all the two-way services, home security is the one that has been most successfully demonstrated to date." In Columbus the penetration rate among cable subscribers for the QUBE security system covering fire, burglary and medical emergencies is 12%. In 1981 this system covered 5000 subscribers' homes, detecting 175 burglaries, 85 fires, 200 requests for medical assistance and 170 requests for emergency assistance.[26] Warner Amex currently offers security services only in Columbus because of lack of demand. In that city 3000 sub-scribers currently have security services on QUBE; several thousand more rely on a cable and telephone link.[27]

The major MSOs in both the United States and Canada are gaining experi-ence with security services. Rogers offers security packages in one of its Cali-fornia systems and in Portland. In addition, its Syracuse experimental system covered 1100 homes and was operational for several years. Based on delivery of a direct notice to fire and police centers, without the intervention of any central monitoring service by Rogers, this system helped to protect privacy by eliminating the cable company's role as middleman. Rogers has produced a low-cost security service which became commercially available in 1983. By August 31, 1983 it had approximately 1000 subscribers. Rogers *does* main-tain an automated data base listing all subscribers to this service.

In 1980 Rogers offered an electronic security system to subscribers in a suburb of Victoria, Canada but lack of sales due to high installation costs led to suspension of the service. In Portland the Rogers' security service will be operated by Brink's Inc., which will offer free installation to subscribers. In addition, Rogers has an experimental license from the CRTC to offer security systems in its franchises in Ontario, British Columbia and Alberta.[28] Another Canadian MSO, Maclean Hunter, is testing home security systems in its Wayne County franchise near Detroit. Telecable Videotron's Vidacom will also include security services.

As usual, opinions are mixed about the economic future of interactive security services. Some Canadian MSOs are only offering the service in their American franchises because of promises made to win a franchise. Others be-lieve that home security is most promising because of increasing consumer concern about burglary. Rogers "anticipates implementation of emergency alarm services in most of its U.S. systems now under construction," and con-cludes that in both the U.S. and Canada "the medium-term outlook for cable alarm services is highly favorable in view of the rapid growth that is currently being experienced in the home security industry."[29] A February 1981 Gallup poll analysis of the intentions of consumers to purchase new home-based technologies found that security equipment was the most popular item; 63% of Ontario respondents intended to make such a purchase to make their "life and property more secure."[30] The London Privacy Survey in December 1982 also found the highest level of respondent interest was for security and emer-gency services.

The Cableguard Example

The Cable Telecommunications Research Institute published an extensive report on the security service, known as Cableguard, operated by Ottawa

Cablevision Limited. The company has encountered significant technical and marketing problems during the start-up phase of this experimental service, and the penetration rate among the limited number of homes to which the service is available is approximately 5% to 6%.[31] The Security Monitoring Agreement between Ottawa Cableguard and the individual subscriber makes no provisions for protecting the confidentiality of subscriber information. (This omission may simply be an effort on the part of the company to avoid liability for breach of confidence by making no promises in its contracts to start with.) The subscriber does authorize Cableguard, fire, medical and police authorities, "having reasonable grounds including the existence of an alarm. . .to enter into and upon the subscriber's premises, in the absence of the subscriber." Cableguard also has the right "in order to verify a computer alert" to "call the subscriber by telephone to request a code response to determine if the set alert is valid and. . .Cableguard shall have the right to record the said telephone call."

As part of the security service agreement with Cableguard, a subscriber has to fill out an authorization schedule that includes the following information: the name, address, telephone number and place of employment of the subscriber; the employment status of the spouse; the names of all residents living at the address; other information, such as the fact that an adult at the residence has a "heart condition," and names to contact in the event of fire and emergency alarms. Cableguard informs subscribers that the information on this latter schedule is available to its "monitoring station operators." The monitoring station also makes a formal written record of any "alarm explanation and follow-up." There is no indication of how long such data are stored.

During the CRTC hearings on non-programming services in Vancouver in April 1981, the chairman of the session, Rosalie Gower, asked George Fierheller how Rogers planned to guarantee the security of personal information provided by subscribers for security services and for opinion-polling. He stated that "you take all the precautions that you reasonably can that this information would not be released to anyone." In Victoria the cable company carefully screens and bonds the persons who work in the security operation, which is located in a locked room. Fierheller admitted that in the Victoria surveillance system, "it would be unrealistic to expect that they [the persons working in the system] wouldn't be able to know on a household basis who was watching what. So again, you've got to be very careful that those people are thoroughly covered for security by bonding, . . .that they won't reveal any of that information. Anything else, of course, would only be on an aggregated basis, if published at all." Government regulations may have to be created to stimulate companies offering security services to assume higher standards of liability for the confidentiality of subscriber data, including provisions for damages in the event of breaches of confidentiality.

Privacy Policies

One major Canadian MSO has in draft form a "subscriber privacy policy" for its operations in the United States and Canada. With respect to security services, this document notes that the nature of the service requires that the name, address, telephone number, type of dwelling and number of persons in the subscriber's household should be retained in computer files: "Depending on the specific services provided, the subscriber may elect to provide names of friends or relatives to be contacted in an emergency and specific medical information as applicable to members of the household." The draft policy notes that the contents of this data file are established with the subscriber in writing prior to the actual commencement of the service. The subscriber may update or modify this file from time to time, and it will be destroyed if the subscriber discontinues the service.

A subscriber to *any* security service does voluntarily furnish certain information about himself or herself, the family and the household. A consumer agrees at the same time to a certain amount of information storage and intrusiveness, because he or she regards the possibility of a burglary or a fire as an even more threatening prospect. An individual thus balances various interests, including the desire for privacy, versus a desire for security protection. However, a subscriber gives up data for a particular purpose only and not for any other uses that might benefit the company alone, such as selling the names of those who can afford security services. A subscriber should also have a contractual right to sue the service provider, if his or her legitimate expectations of confidentiality are not met.

Potential Problems

Some potential privacy problems clearly exist in the use of security services. The two-way system permits continuous monitoring of movements in and out of the home, unless the alarm system is turned off. When a subscriber returns to a wired home, he or she has a few seconds to punch a security code into the terminal keypad before an alarm sounds. If that happens, then the monitoring station investigates, initially by telephone, and may record the conversation. Thus the personnel at the headend computer would know that a subscriber is unable on a regular basis to enter the security code in his home, because he is under an alcoholic influence, for example.

This situation is of course no different for an alarm service that uses some other medium of communication, and inherent privacy problems are similar to those posed by the use of two-way security systems.

A subscriber has to decide whether or not any loss of privacy is involved in furnishing personal information to a security system for emergency use.

The element of voluntariness and balancing of interests involved in furnishing such information is a good form of protection for personal privacy, at least for this specialized type of consumer service.

Different privacy problems will have to be faced if security services are not handled by a cable or telephone company but by an affiliated company or a specialized service, at least to the extent that subscriber data will flow to service providers standing outside the direct linkage between the cable or telephone company and the user, and there is likely to be more duplication in the keeping of identifiable individual records. The system operators in this case will have to ensure that their policies on privacy and security are applied to the third parties.

Profile of a Two-Way Cable Security System

In closing this section on security services, it is worthwhile to examine the practices of Selkirk Communications Ltd., a Canadian company which operates the only two-way service in the state of Florida through its subsidiary, Selkirk Communications Inc. of Fort Lauderdale. (The parent company operates in a variety of areas in Canada, the United States and the United Kingdom, including radio, television and cable; the largest single shareholder is Southam Inc. of Toronto. Selkirk owns approximately one-half of the major cable companies in Winnipeg and Ottawa. The latter company, Ottawa Cablevision Ltd., operates the Cableguard system. Selkirk also owns a 37.7% equity interest in Tocom Inc. in the U.S. and all of Tocom Canada Ltd. Tocom manufactures the technical equipment used in the security systems in Ottawa and Fort Lauderdale, thus again illustrating the possibilities of hardware manufacturers and cable or telephone operators combining to promote the use of two-way services.)

Selkirk won the franchise for Fort Lauderdale and five other local communities in July 1978, partly because it was the only company capable of delivering the two-way services desired by the local authorities. Its cable system, including security services, has been serving customers since July 1979. The company had 46,000 subscribers in 1983 and has a potential market of 115,000 homes. It hopes to achieve a penetration rate for the security system of 10% to 15% of serviced homes.

The Fort Lauderdale security system uses a home terminal that is comparable to an addressable converter with a return response capacity. The headend computer can sweep as many as 64,000 homes with a polling signal every six seconds. If an alarm sounds, the computer prints out the specific name, type of alarm, directions for the fire department and any other pertinent data furnished by the subscriber, such as the number of persons living in the home and the specific location of bedrooms. A subscriber can also choose to furnish additional medical information to Selkirk Security Systems, which can be given to paramedics on their way to the scene.

Selkirk does not offer any other two-way service in Fort Lauderdale. It regards itself as primarily a supplier of home entertainment and operates so that other activities, such as the security service, do not interfere with the primary goal. It does not conduct any channel monitoring, because such activity can potentially be perceived as consumer surveillance. Selkirk believes that the biggest problem in introducing any two-way service is persuading consumers to change their patterns of doing things, especially the group that is already over 40.

Selkirk has six separate local franchise agreements, which include statements about the confidentiality of personal information, such as a requirement that the company not release a list of names of subscribers. The subscribers enter into a security system agreement, which primarily binds the customer. None of the 24 clauses in the agreement bind the company to protect the confidentiality of personal information acquired from a household during the course of operations. Clause 16 requires the customer to acknowledge "that it is impractical and extremely difficult to fix the damages, if any, which may proximately result from the failure of COMPANY to perform its obligation hereunder or which may result from the failure of the System to operate. . . ." The company's liability for liquidated damages is then fixed at $200. In Clause 23 the "CUSTOMER acknowledges that the System is constantly monitored by the System computer to determine operational status and alarm status and agrees that COMPANY may utilize such status information for any legitimate purpose."

The security system agreement in Fort Lauderdale is thus deficient, in my opinion, in protecting the confidentiality of personal information pertaining to subscribers, even if management is fully aware of the importance of privacy and confidentiality.

Conclusion

Thus, significant privacy problems exist for the subscriber, whether personal data are centralized at the headend computer of the cable or telephone company or simply transmitted on a transactional basis to the provider of the service. Security services furnish a comprehensive method of keeping a particular home under continued surveillance. It is not difficult to imagine how police, security and private detective agencies will attempt to benefit from such an existing system, especially by obtaining informal access to the resulting data pool.[32]

PUBLIC OPINION-POLLING

On December 30, 1981 the CRTC described an opinion-polling service as follows: "This is a form of monitoring service which would permit a wide scope of new initiatives ranging from simple expression of opinion to such matters as a sampling of political opinions, election surveys or the polling of community views on legislation and a variety of other matters of civic or community interest."[33] Using the keypad attached to a television set, a respondent can directly express his or her opinion on a question that is posed on the TV program being viewed. Responses are generally limited to a yes or no format or a choice of several replies listed on the TV screen. One of the asserted goals of the cable companies is to make television more interactive, more responsible and more interesting than the passive mechanism that it has been to date.[34]

Most of the major MSOs in the U.S. and Canada have polling experiments or services in place. In Columbus QUBE offers an interactive viewer response system, especially on its "Columbus Live" channel. It has included polling on such sensitive questions as knowledge of homosexuals. In May 1983 Warner Amex inaugurated a two-way service on the QUBE network allowing 180,000 viewers in six cities to express their opinions instantly about programs and advertising. An hour-and-a-half of programs were open to viewer participation. Advertisers were able to test products and develop strategies for their sales. (Although Warner Amex expected to have 1 million subscribers to its weekly QUBE Network by 1990, the company decided in January 1984 to cancel the network for financial reasons.)[35]

In a limited number of homes in London, Ontario, the opinions of a sample of households on a particular issue can be recorded and compiled instantaneously for voting and sampling purposes. The experiment in London seems typical of the current state of development of interactive cable services. Equipment for this two-way system was installed in 300 homes and was used to record respondents' preferences on a number of issues. The system has not been used for several years, although Rogers Cable TV Ltd. is in the process of reviving the test.

The London Rogers outlet wisely designed its polling experiment with careful attention to informed consent. From the start, the company asked for volunteers, all of whom signed a document indicating their willingness to participate. Each home was contacted in advance of each voting episode and offered an opportunity to withdraw from the particular test. No one did withdraw, which is a reminder that some people are quite prepared to give up some privacy in order to be noticed, and indeed taken account of, in an increasingly depersonalized society.

The 300 homes in the Rogers public opinion-polling sample are all located in the same neighborhood. At least seven or eight experiments were conducted, and all the product was statistical in character. Currently, Rogers does not intend to expand the two-way system until the revived economy permits it to generate more revenue. Since the system is already interactive in each of the 300 homes, the company can tell what channel is being watched in each home.[36]

CRTC Recommendations

In its December 30, 1981 granting of licenses, the CRTC established a number of preconditions for offering opinion-polling services in Canada. It wisely recognized that the principle of informed consent was essential: "Subscribers would give their prior consent to participate in any such service." Because intervenors in the CRTC hearings had become concerned about the dangers of putting such a vast amount of information in the hands of cable companies, "the applicants confirmed that they would take all necessary precautions to ensure adequate safeguards to protect subscribers' privacy and security."

> In the Commission's view these monitoring services could give rise to serious social concerns if such safeguards were not carefully applied. In light of the implications relating to the security of information and to invasion of privacy, the Commission will only allow the cable distribution of such services if it is satisfied that proper mechanisms and safeguards are put in place. . . .Approval of the opinion-polling service is conditional upon licensees obtaining the prior agreement of each subscriber to be polled and, where appropriate, upon periodic or specific alerts being incorporated into the service to advise such subscribers that monitoring is being performed. Further, the Commission expects cable television licensees, when announcing the results of a particular poll, to take every precaution to identify clearly the limitations of the survey in order to help subscribers to interpret the results adequately.[37]

The CRTC offered no further detailed guidelines reflecting the types of safeguards necessary to effectively protect the privacy and security of subscriber information.

Necessary Protections

In the QUBE system in Columbus only a limited number of staff employees know how to conduct surveys or access polling information. The director of programs has to approve all polls in advance. Each viewer is informed about each particular poll and given a chance to participate or withdraw.[38]

Any company offering an opinion-polling service should insist that the permission of the subscriber has to be obtained in advance of his or her participation. To a significant extent, this leaves it up to the individual sub-scriber to decide on the protection of his or her own privacy, whether the activity involves the expression of a point of view on a particular issue, or a situation in which the respondent makes a choice that is recorded and stored in identifiable form. One further relevant protection for an individual in opinion-polling is that the company will only know the response by house-hold, unless a person lives alone or new technology allows particular respon-dents to identify themselves.

A desirable additional protection is that subscribers should have the right to drop out of an opinion survey at any point. At the Vancouver CRTC hear-ings one Commission member raised the issue of the privacy of individuals in opinion-polling. George Fierheller responded as follows:

> Well, certainly one way to protect privacy, of course, is obviously to ask people for their permission. And they don't even, having given permission, they don't necessarily reply to any particular question if they don't feel they want to. It's a purely discretionary sort of thing on their part. In terms of protection then, the whole operation would very quickly fall apart, as indeed would Statistics Canada or any other collection organization for this kind of data if, in fact, there were ever leaks from it that ever identified individual informa-tion with a particular householder. So it would be to the advantage of the polling company and everyone else to make sure that this didn't happen.[39]

The difference between a cable company and Statistics Canada is that the Statistics Act creates a burden of strict criminal and civil liability for any un-lawful release of personal information in identifiable form by the national statistical agency or one of its employees.[40] No criminal liability would currently accompany such an occurrence involving a cable company in Canada, since there is no statutory obligation. Its civil liability under the common law would probably depend on the consumer's ability to demon-strate negligence on the part of the company or its employees, resulting in harm to the interests of the subscriber.

Data Storage

Although the principle of requiring the individual subscriber's informed consent is widely accepted, there seems to be less consensus on whether or not the data collected by polling subscribers' opinions on a particular issue should or will be stored. Rogers and Maclean Hunter cable systems in place and in the design stage in Canada and the U.S. are not constructed so as to allow for storage or recovery of data on a particular individual. The same is true for the QUBE system in Columbus. But the important point is that the software *could* be designed in such a way that individual opinions were stored and retrievable.[41] The use of a two-way cable system for opinion-polling makes it very easy to store individual opinions automatically, just as a radio phone-in show can tape record the views of callers.

Current Policies

Perhaps because subscriber privacy is so obviously capable of being jeopardized in opinion-polling, cable companies in the U.S. and Canada have done an excellent job of formulating policies designed to prevent privacy infringements in the operation of such services. The Warner Amex Code of Privacy states that its subscriber agreements shall include the following:

> A. Individual subscriber viewing or responses may be recognized only where necessary to permit billing or to render a subscriber service. Any such information will be kept strictly confidential unless publication is an inherent part of the service (e.g., announcing a game show prize winner).

> B. No other individualized information concerning viewing or responses will be developed unless the subscriber has been advised in advance and given adequate opportunity not to participate.

This agreement extends to services beyond opinion-polling. The subscriber contract for the Columbus QUBE system provides that "a Subscriber would have the opportunity to interact with QUBE programming as, for example, by registering opinions, ordering programs and other products, and participating in game and other shows. Such interaction is entirely voluntary and is completely within Subscriber's own control."[42]

The draft subscriber privacy policy of one major Canadian MSO provides that in any type of interactive programming "responses made by subscribers to the service will be tabulated numerically. The publicly announced or published results will be presented in absolute numbers and percentages and will not include any data identifying the individual." The 1981 municipal franchise ordinance under which Rogers operates in Portland, OR also contains a section (13.6) on polling by cable:

> No polls or other two-way responses of subscribers shall be conducted unless the program of which the poll is a part shall contain an explicit disclosure of the nature, purpose, and prospective use of the results of the poll. No commercial or other use of the information of subscriber viewing habits or patterns may be made and no release of such information shall be permitted without the prior consent of the Grantor [Portland] or pursuant to rules and regulations duly adopted by the Grantor.

Additional Privacy Problems in Opinion-Polling

Some additional privacy problems in opinion-polling deserve brief mention. Section 5 of the January 20, 1982 notice of inquiry of the State of New York Commission on Cable Television notes that "opinion polling, although it has value in certain respects, would involve the storage of information which a person may well prefer to remain private." As in the discussion above of channel monitoring services, the actual storage of individual information derived from public opinion-polling might increase the pressure on cable companies to maximize their economic return from such information resources. Companies offering two-way services possess a great deal of personal information that would be of significant benefit to marketing firms. During the Toronto CRTC hearings in March 1981 John Graham, the chairman of Rogers, mentioned that in the London, Ontario public opinion-polling experiment "we had not contemplated selling, if you will, the results of polls of that kind. At the same time, you might have specially commissioned ones if things evolved in a sufficiently sophisticated manner to enable that to be done." The American Civil Liberties Union in Columbus, OH has pointed out that there is nothing to prevent QUBE from selling information on the opinions of viewers. The response from Warner Amex is that it does not register information obtained through opinion-polling, which is, of course, a desirable practice. A polling system, however, makes it possible for subscribers voluntarily to indicate their interest in a particular product or subject, thus making their own decision on a privacy issue.

The discussion earlier in this chapter about channel monitoring services mentioned problems of group privacy that emerge in the collection of personal data in two-way services. The QUBE polling system in Ohio permits the restriction of viewer response to only a small area of the city, so that a town meeting, for example, can be held on the system for only a specific locality.[43] Thus, the opinions of a small area of a city might be publicized to the possible detriment of individuals living in that particular area.

Interactive public opinion-polling raises other sensitive issues that should not be confused with concern for personal privacy. Whether cable companies allow opinion surveys of any sort on their systems, for example, does not directly affect the privacy of individuals concerned. Households can turn off their television sets or refuse to participate or to answer specific questions. The same action can be taken by the subscriber if a cable company or a user of an opinion–polling service asks sensitive questions, such as ones dealing with sexual preferences or political views. Cable companies are designing two-way opinion-polling facilities for use by special interest groups, who will formulate the questions. A public interest provision in U.S. law requires a cable company to grant access to an interest group for such purposes. Privacy issues only arise in this case if individuals choose to answer questions about politics, religion or sexual practices, for example, and the cable company then stores the individual information in identifiable form; such a practice can and should be avoided.

TELE-EDUCATION

Tele-education simply refers to the use of interactive systems for educational purposes. Experiments in using various types of communications systems for educational purposes are taking place all over North America. Videotron in Montreal already offers one-channel service solely for tele-education, but it is a one-way service. Its plans for two-way systems include education. The CRTC approved Videotron's plan to distribute "a service consisting of training and refresher courses developed by professional associations for the exclusive use of their membership."[44]

Tele-education courses in Ottawa use the cable and the telephone, but the interactive capability is little used by the students. The University Hospital in London, Ontario has tele-education and tele-health experiments in progress between London and the neighboring town of Woodstock, using a satellite for interactive transmissions.[45] The two-way system operated by Rogers in Portland will be offered to educators for use in courses. This plan is based on an experiment in Rockford, IL, where firemen received training courses in their homes in order to reduce the amount of time spent away from their families.

Warner Amex appears to be the leader in developing tele-education courses. Interactive systems in Columbus, Cincinnati and Pittsburgh are linking QUBE subscribers with classrooms at Ohio State University and the Columbus Technical Institute. A spokesman for the company said that half a dozen other cities may soon have the capability. According to an article in the August 15, 1982 Montreal *Sunday Express,* "a viewer tuned in on a college classroom in progress is given the capability of raising his electronic hand simply by punching a button that instantly identifies him to the teacher and indicates that he has a question. The question then is relayed to the teacher by a telephone hooked up to a speaker phone and dealt with for the benefit of both students in the classroom and in the viewing audience." If the classroom in question is located within an area wired into the QUBE system, then the transmission from student to teacher can occur by means of cable.

The obvious privacy question that arises with tele-education is the extent to which interactive systems store the individual responses to questions posed by an educator. It cannot be so readily argued, as in the case of opinion-polling, that software systems should be designed in such a manner as to make it impossible for an individual response to be recorded, since in an educational system it may be necessary for the instructor to know, at least temporarily, whether or not a correct response has been received and from which student.

This is the case in tele-education services offered by the Rogers system in Portland. Although it is possible to separate the software for opinion-polling from the software used for a tele-education course, the result would involve complex engineering maneuvers, which nevertheless may be desirable for protecting personal privacy.[46]

TELESHOPPING

The introductory statement to the CRTC's experimental licenses for non-programming services on December 30, 1981 defined teleshopping as a system that would "offer interested subscribers what, in effect, is an electronic catalog retrieval service enabling subscribers to view, select and order merchandise directly from their homes or businesses. The service would be provided by retail stores, distributors and others." The carrying capacity of cable is such that several catalogs' worth of information from a large number of stores could be accommodated on a single television channel.[47]

Selected retailers find teleshopping very attractive as a way of obtaining customer orders at the push of a button, and a great many experimental systems are in place in Western Europe and North America. West Germany conducted a teleshopping and telebanking trial involving 4000 homes. In the United Kingdom the Prestel videotex service combines the use of a television set with a telephone for purposes of teleshopping. The government of Margaret Thatcher and editorial writers in *The Economist* foresee a very promising future for teleshopping and telebanking after Great Britain has been wired for cable.[48]

Telecable Videotron is licensed by the CRTC to offer teleshopping on an experimental basis in the province of Quebec. Its current plans to place terminals in 100,000 homes are largely inspired by the goal of achieving a teleshopping system for its subscribers in several cities and towns. Rogers is licensed to offer teleshopping on an experimental basis in Ontario, British Columbia and Alberta. At the time of the CRTC's non-programming service hearings in the spring of 1981, Rogers had already held discussions involving teleshopping with Eatons, Canadian Tire and Woodwards. Company executives explained that "the product can be ordered directly using the same keypad as is used on a pay TV wonderbox. We believe very strongly in one box being used for a number of services in order to keep the cost down." Rogers stated that telephone companies and Simpson-Sears have a similar audio-shopping service: "It operates with push-button telephones directly ordering into a computer. Our proposal would be a vastly superior service because it's video." In Vancouver a Rogers executive explained that teleshopping would involve the use of a personal identification code and payment by means of a credit card or charge account card.[49] Rogers is currently offering a service known as Cableshop on two of its local California systems. A subscriber uses a telephone to order a pre-selected commercial on a product, which is then delivered to the household via cable television. The next step will permit ordering of a product by cable or telephone.

Bell Canada has been actively developing a teleshopping service combining Telidon videotex technology with the use of the telephone as a delivery system. Hudson's Bay Company of Winnipeg introduced video shopping to customers in its downtown Winnipeg store using two Telidon terminals accessing 300 pages from its catalogs. A telephone/television set teleshopping service is also available to farmers in Western Canada from Hudson's Bay Company on the Grassroots interactive system; it is operated by Infomart of Toronto.[50]

The most promising teleshopping experiment involves Infomart and Consumers Distributing Company Limited using the Bell Canada Vista project, a videotex field test. Consumers in Toronto are being offered goods for sale directly through television terminals using Telidon. Users can actually order goods through the system rather than simply view information. The service is available in 225 Toronto homes. The technology "permits a viewer at any time to dial up graphic displays and information about anything available in the system."[51] Goods can then be ordered via push-button telephones and charged on credit cards.

A great many teleshopping ventures exist in the United States using various media.[52] Times Mirror Cable ran a trial of The Shopping Channel in six cable franchises serving 150,000 subscribers. Viewers could order merchandise by calling Comp-U-Card's toll-free number. The latter also offers a shopping service using a personal computer, known as Comp-U-Star, which various cable operators are testing. The Cableshop service uses the Peabody, MA cable system to advertise products, which are then ordered by telephone. Although this small cable system has interactive capability, it is not used for the Cableshop service. Cableshop, however, does allow viewers to use a special telephone number to order the specific product message that they are interested in seeing. All of these services may be forerunners of truly interactive shopping services available by cable or telephone. Both Warner Amex's QUBE service and Cox Cable's Index service are developing two-way capacity for teleshopping.

Teleshopping is a good example of a two-way service for which a cable or telephone company might simply provide the transmission system. In practice, the company would lease its equipment and a channel to a number of retailers. The headend computers would be used for transactional purposes only and might not store records on individuals, once verification of the customer's identity had occurred. A cable company might have to keep a log of the transaction in order to protect against any claims made by service providers. As suggested earlier, the headend computers might not even be capable of storing this much transactional information for any substantial length of time. In a computerized shopping service operated in the United States by Comp-U-Star, transactional information is kept on active tapes for billing purposes and then dumped onto inactive tapes for three years as required by law.[53] Such a practice would be useful in restricting unauthorized and third-party access to personal information, since inactive tapes are harder to access.

During the Vancouver CRTC hearings in April 1981 there were a number of discussions involving the extent to which a cable company would control the use of such a shared channel. George Fierheller suggested that the ultimate responsibility for controlling such a channel rests with the CRTC: "We obviously would have to live within whatever guidelines are provided, given the fact that we are a broadcasting undertaking and given the fact that we are responsible to ensure that we do not do things that will adversely affect the broadcast industry. So...I think the ultimate control really rests with the CRTC to put on whatever rules and regulations they feel will be necessary to protect the broadcaster." A Commission member noted that access to the teleshopping channel would involve a contract between the cable company and the user. However, the ultimate responsibility for protecting the confidentiality of consumer information under such circumstances needs to be established, preferably including shared liability between the system operator and the service provider.

At first glance the kinds of planned teleshopping systems using cable and the telephone are no different from the telephone shopping operations currently run by major retailers in the United States and Canada. However, a fully interactive system using cable would mean that teleshopping data could be integrated into a total profile of the subscriber, if a company stores the appropriate individual information. This is a general problem with two-way systems that will be returned to later in this chapter. Once again, we must take note of the economic and marketing pressures in the direction of using such consumer information. Indeed, an article in the September 25, 1981 issue of *The Wall Street Journal* noted that marketing people regard teleshopping as "an aid in accumulating the data needed to track buying habits." Therefore, information on consumer purchasing patterns used in conjunction with other individualized data could provide cable companies with a valuable and much sought-after commodity.

TELEBANKING

Telebanking is a service by which a subscriber using a keypad, television set and the cable or telephone system can conduct such transactions as finding out checking account balances, moving funds between accounts and paying bills to various companies.

The expectations for implementing home banking are very high. Almost 50% of the largest American banks would like "on-line bank at home services," while a recent survey in the U.S., conducted by Payment Systems Inc., found home banking to be the most desired two-way service among consumers. A 1981 survey of national operations/automation by the American Bankers Association found that consumers had very high expectations that home banking using the television set would become a reality after 1984.[54] Another recent survey of new services conducted by Reymer and Gersin Associates of New York indicated that the general public favored telebanking over other prospective offerings. It is, of course, not certain that cable will win out over other types of delivery services for home banking. But it is evident that the banks themselves have a significant interest in developing such services both as a convenience and as one way of controlling the costs of doing business. Moreover, an entrepreneur like John Kelly, chairman of the board of the Nabu group of companies, argues that "there will be a revolution in how routine things are done. The realities of teleshopping and telebanking are with us today."[55]

QUBE has plans for telebanking in Columbus, but as of mid-1984 the system was not used for home banking. In its franchising proposals in Sacramento, CA and Montgomery County, MD, Maclean Hunter included telebanking in the list of promised interactive services. This is one instance where Maclean Hunter is promising more than Rogers in the form of two-way services; the latter is not offering telebanking at present in its American franchises. The Bank of Montreal started a commercial home banking service in November 1983 for about 2000 subscribers to Grassroots, the Infomart videotex service operating in Manitoba, Alberta and Ontario. Users are able to check account balances, transfer funds from one account to another and review monthly statements on their television screens.[56]

Rogers is still planning an experiment in telebanking in Vancouver, but appropriate agreements have not yet been concluded with Nabu Network Corp., which is to be the service provider. Subscribers to this service would use a keypad in the home during off-hours to move money around in their accounts. The transactions would be done on a standby computer and then checked during regular banking hours. At the CRTC hearings in Vancouver in April 1981, Harry Davis, the engineer in charge of this experiment, described the process as follows: "Using an interactive hand control, the subscriber will input a special personal identification number to gain access to his or her records. Then, knowing the account numbers, the subscriber can interrogate the off-line system for such things as account balance inquiries, interest rate information, internal account transfers of funds and later complete bill payments. An additional level of security will be required, of course, within our plant to ensure privacy of transmission." The Rogers experiment is an imitation of a system developed by Bank One in Columbus, which "operates on a one-day delay so that an audit can occur before inserting the transaction into the on-line banking system."

In November 1983 the Knight-Ridder newspaper chain introduced the first commercial telebanking service in the U.S. on its Viewtron videotex system in southeastern Florida. Consumers have to purchase a Sceptre terminal and pay monthly service charges to the local telephone company and to Viewtron. In cooperation with several regional banks in Florida, Ohio, North Carolina and California, the company plans to introduce the service in 17 cities within about two years.

Several Americans banks, such as Chemical Bank of New York and Shawmut Corp. in eastern Massachusetts, are offering home banking services at present on a commercial basis. Customers may bank and pay bills from their homes or offices, using a personal computer, a telephone and a modem (the latter allows a computer to transmit and receive data over a telephone).[57]

Telebanking intensifies the normal problems of protecting privacy and confidentiality in electronic banking systems.[58] Some cable companies suggest that banks and their customers will have to look after their own privacy interests. At least a few banks and trust companies do not see any unusual privacy implications in these proposed interactive services and argue that no one is interested in privacy. At one level, the headend computer of the company offering the service will, of course, intervene in the standard relationship between the bank and the customer. On the other hand, access to one's bank account from a home terminal is not much different from access by automated teller; either option necessitates suitable precautions in the interests of confidentiality and security.

Specific Privacy Issues Raised by Telebanking

In 1978 the U.S. Right to Financial Privacy Act "declared that individuals have a right to privacy in their bank accounts, and spelled out some of the duties as to confidentiality and disclosure required of bank officials."

The American privacy expert, Alan F. Westin, subsequently discussed the privacy implications of in-home banking in a superb article.[59] Although he focuses on the situation in the U.S., some of his comments also have direct relevance to Canada, where there is no statutory protection for the confidentiality of personal information in banking systems. Westin drew a very pertinent conclusion from the Sentry Insurance/Louis Harris 1979 survey of public and leadership attitudes towards privacy. Most commercial bankers are "at odds with the public on privacy issues in general and more out of step than other industry executives (in insurance, employment, etc.) in relation to privacy issues affecting their particular clientele. In addition, the survey showed that most bankers want to wait until the law dictates what should be done to protect depositor privacy, rather than pioneer such policies voluntarily, in keeping with what consumers want." Westin also points out that "while some leading banks have issued voluntary customer privacy rules, most commercial banks have still not adopted the important privacy policies recommended by the 1977 Privacy Commission report."

Westin predicts "that within the next 20 years we will have installed in probably a majority of homes the capacity to engage in financial transactions (including loans) by telecommunications from a home device, whether cable TV, home computer, or telephone instrument." He suggests that these systems to be used for financial transactions will be part of a total two-way interactive system, such as we have been discussing in this chapter. Westin wisely observes that privacy problems will be most serious when "combinations of financial and non-financial organizations unite to own and manage the home systems," and "the equipment and lines of these systems are used for handling data of varying degrees of sensitivity and by many data managers." Thus he foresees major rather than limited privacy problems to be faced in the future.

Westin identifies four major privacy issues which may arise in connection with telebanking. The first involves limits on data storage:

> If data about the individual's movements, financial transactions, consumer choices, and other information are permanently stored—then there will be many arguments by government regulators, commercial marketeers, researchers, and other interests that these data should not be destroyed—a pool of revealing personal information almost without precedent will be created: it will have to be protected against unauthorized use. Issue number one, therefore, is whether home banking will be able to be made a system of largely transient rather than permanent data.

Secondly, Westin points to the need for careful measures of security, including the use of encryption, to ensure that sensitive personal information is kept confidential. Thirdly, he points out that at present we "secure much protection of privacy from this fracturing of our personal information into independent organizational pigeonholes." The creation of integrated master profiles for all kinds of purposes will have to be resisted; the risks of this occurring are particularly severe as financial institutions integrate their data bases on individuals in order to promote the sale of a variety of consumer services. Finally, there are significant problems in determining how to control third-party access to consumer data collected by interactive services:

> ...the questions will be what criminal activity or government program purposes will be considered important enough for the home data bases and network to be breached, who will make that determination, under what standards of weighing personal privacy against claimed public interest, and with what safeguards as to the scope of inspection or surveillance? Pressures by government may become very intense as problems of terrorism, social protest, illegal immigra-

tion, and fraud in benefit programs spur legislators to seek access to home consumer data.

Westin concludes that "these four issues represent central privacy questions that home banking trends will require us to answer." In fact, these issues are crucial for all electronic consumer services.

Westin recommends that leading individual American banks ought to create privacy task forces to formulate voluntary privacy policies "applied in pilot and experimental projects, in tests of these policies in operation." His views have direct relevance as well to the information-handling activities of all companies offering interactive services.

One Bank's Approach

The Bank of Montreal has been first among Canadian banks in publishing its policies on the protection of customers' privacy; its initiatives set at least a basic level of appropriate behavior for companies involved in telebanking. The bank sums up its privacy principles as follows: "We ask only the minimum of personal information required to handle your business with us. Access to that material is strictly controlled. We do not give information about you to the government, unless authorized by you or required by law. We maintain on file no more information than we need." In terms of government access to information, the bank complies with statutory obligations, such as income tax laws, to furnish certain data to the government: "Beyond that, requests from government agencies for information are turned down unless, as in the case of court actions, they are accompanied by a subpoena or warrant." Requests for access to customer information by other third parties "are rejected unless they are accompanied by a court order."[60] Companies offering interactive services should apply these same principles to all of their information-handling activities about subscribers.

At its own insistence, the Bank of Montreal is responsible for the confidentiality of personal banking data on the Grassroots telebanking service for farmers. Infomart, the operator of the system, furnishes the bank with a switch or gateway* to subscribers, but apparently retains no record of individual banking transactions.

INFORMATION RETRIEVAL

An operational two-way cable or telephone system permits subscribers to order up pages of information to be delivered on the television screen by using a device in the home or office that allows the viewer to access a data

---

*A form of direct computer access.

bank for information on a particular subject. All kinds of data can ultimately be delivered to and from the individual home, including electronic mail, messages and newspapers.

Here, as elsewhere, a distinction needs to be drawn between the provider of the service and the carrier. In some instances the cable company, for example, may serve as both the information provider and the carrier; in other instances the company will simply act as the carrier and will lease the channel to a service provider. This practice raises issues not only of competition and of controlling access to a delivery system but also of personal privacy, because of the sharing of information that could occur. At the June 1981 Hull hearings of the CRTC, Andre Chagnon of Telecable Videotron emphasized that his company was "not the information provider." It "will lease channels to third parties for the provision of these non-programming services." Although Chagnon meant this statement to apply to all of the interactive services offered by his company, it has particular application to the practice of information retrieval. At the CRTC hearings in Vancouver, Peter S. Grant, a leading communications lawyer, intervened on behalf of the Canadian Daily Newspaper Publishers Association. Its main concern was "the need to ensure that potential information providers are treated fairly and without discrimination in their dealings with the cable licensee." In Grant's view there would be no problem if the cable industry acted solely as a carrier, which is of course unlikely.[61]

At the Toronto March 1981 CRTC hearings, Rogers emphasized that its information services on two-way cable would be provided by such organizations as Infomart, Canadian Press, Info-Globe, Reuters, financial institutions and others: "A module of the pay TV wonderbox will decode the service which will otherwise be digitally encoded and thus unwatchable to all the cable connected subscribers." An expansion of such information services could provide a subscriber owning a home computer with software and computer programming delivered via cable: "Subscribers could, with their home computers, access central computers for translation services, electronic message services, scheduling, participation in interactive education courses, obtaining external data bases such as the Source, Compu-Serve and the stock market."

Rogers went on to explain that its information-providing services would follow the lead of Telecable Videotron. The extraordinary carrying capacity of the latter's Vidacom system indicates its market potential:

It will, for example, have the technical capacity to transmit more than 1000 pages of text in one second, and up to 20,000 pages in a single cycle. These pages could be drawn from material stored in a data bank. The user could access these pages by punching 'menus' or lists of items, indexes, or selected pages or papers, and code in his or her request for one or more page subjects. Retrieval will take an average of less than two seconds, regardless of the number of active users, with certain data accessible only to those who subscribe for it. The computer-stored information can be updated continuously. . . . in addition, the system will provide the delivery of user-selected material, by inserting these pages in one of the cycles at the proper time.[62]

The Vidacom system will use Telidon's videotex process as the method of delivery. It should be noted, however, that this description of Vidacom reflects plans rather than working reality; designing and producing an operating two-way system are two different things.

A number of the information-delivery systems that are currently in place in the U.S. and Canada are one-way downstream. For example, Videotron is currently producing an electronic newspaper with *La Presse* of Montreal. The one-way Reuters IDR cable service, which is carried by a number of cable systems in North America, primarily offers business information for selected commercial users on a fee basis.[63]

A surprising number of information retrieval services is already available using home computers and telephone links. It seems almost inevitable that these general information delivery systems, whatever the communication medium used, will eventually become even more tailored to the immediate needs of individual household and business users, who can indicate specifically what information they want from any particular data base. For example, the Dow Alert is a customized news service being marketed to home and office radios in Boston and Philadelphia by coded signals sent from satellites to FM stations. The subscriber indicates what news he or she wishes to receive and only that information is beamed into the particular home or office.[64]

At least one cable company critic has suggested that there is not much of a future for information retrieval services on cable, since the monthly cost to subscribers would be substantial for materials that individuals are accustomed to obtaining far more cheaply from other sources. On the other hand, Terry Shepard, executive director of the Cable Telecommunications Research Institute in Ottawa, expects that cable systems will gradually enter the data communications market, first with business customers and later in homes. The services will include access to computer programs, games and data bases, and two-way communications.[65] Rogers is currently offering access to information in its Portland system.

Some very innovative work is occurring in Ottawa, where Nabu Manufacturing Corp. and Ottawa Cablevision scored a data communications first in March 1982 "by transmitting a number of video games software packages" through the cable line from the cable company's central computer to certain homes in Ottawa. Nabu plans to make more than 300 software programs available to U.S. and Canadian cable companies. In addition to games, word-processing and business accounting packages will be offered for conventional minicomputers. Nabu has also developed a home microcomputer that hooks up to cable television.[66]

In January 1984 Nabu Manufacturing Corp. split into two main components, one of which, Nabu Network Corp., is pursuing the goal of renting computing software on a monthly subscription basis to home consumers on North American cable systems. Rogers plans to have major trials of the Nabu Network in place in Vancouver and Toronto by the end of 1984. On May 1, 1984 the Nabu Network became available in Ottawa from both Skyline Cablevision Ltd. and Ottawa Cablevision Ltd. The software service and the home computer are also available in Alexandria, Virginia. Campeau Corp. of Toronto, a major Canadian development company, now owns 53.4% of Nabu Network. Moreover, Thomas Wheeler, the eight-year president of the U.S. National Cable Television Association, has joined Nabu Network. Nevertheless, the future of this home cable service remains in doubt.[67]

Privacy Problems

Violations of privacy in the use of information retrieval systems will particularly arise if consumers use a two-way system to order specific pieces of information and a record is made of the contents of the request. In addition, identifiable data will be collected on the consumer, if a specific charge is imposed for each item of information that is ordered. The proposed policy for the information retrieval service of one major Canadian multi-system operator provides that "information retrieval services will be provided on a monthly or time-of-use billing basis. Subscribers must provide written authorization to the Company prior to the Company's compilation or storage of any lists of individual items or pages referenced." This kind of arrangement would be of great benefit in protecting the confidentiality of information retrieved by specific subscribers.

Cable and telephone companies will have to be encouraged to provide information retrieval services in such a way that no record is created of the specific information accessed by particular individuals. However, it seems likely that general information retrieval services will have to impose charges on a page-by-page basis, which will increase the need for individualized record-keeping. Apparently Infomart does charge on a page-by-page basis for information retrieved from the systems it serves as an information provider. In the Bell Vista system, for example, Vista received a printout each week of who had been accessing information; identities of individuals were coded to prevent third-party identification. Infomart uses the data on information retrieved on its videotex systems for internal reports and analyses only. Such protective policies and measures need to be further developed.

VIDEOTEX

Videotex refers to the transmission of textual data for display on a video screen. There are two distinct forms of videotex—teletext and viewdata. Teletext is a one-way system in which the data "piggybacks" the normal broadcast signal, making use of what is known as the "vertical blanking interval," and can be viewed on specially adapted TV sets. Viewdata is an interactive system in which the viewer's television is interconnected via phone lines, cable or microwave with a central computer data bank. For our purposes, we use the word videotex to refer to viewdata, a technology by which any of the interactive services discussed above can be delivered. Since videotex has attracted so much attention and can use such a variety of transmission mediums, it is discussed separately here.

Both cable and telephone-based videotex systems produce similar problems of protecting confidentiality and privacy. Videotex itself has in fact received much more public attention to date than two-way cable television, except perhaps for the QUBE experiment in Columbus. In Western Europe and in North America a great many videotex experiments have been taking place for several years. Although predictions about its market prospects range from unbounded optimism to cautious pessimism, the future of videotex technology seems quite positive, in part because it can be used with both cable and telephone.[68]

Videotex technology has attracted considerable publicity in Canada because of the strong commitment of the federal Department of Communications to Telidon, which is a "coding technique" for a technical link between data format and video format. This Canadian videotex system can be either one-way or two-way. The Vidacom system of Telecable Videotron in Quebec is using Telidon technology in a 250-terminal experiment. The state of the art in videotex is very much in flux, and a system like Telidon may disappear in time. Although the federal government continues to promote Telidon, Lawrence Surtees aptly described the current situation when he wrote in *The Globe and Mail* on January 13, 1984 that "like a ship without an anchor, Telidon is adrift in the absence of content geared to the specific needs of users. A constant criticism of the medium is that it is a technology in search of a job."

The method of delivery known as videotex can be either telephone-based, over-the-air or cable-based. The Prestel videotex system in the United Kingdom currently uses a telephone and a TV set. Videotex generally includes a retrieval service that is two-way, is transmitted by cable TV or telephone lines, and through which consumers can respond to information they receive by answering questions or ordering merchandise. Videotex systems have the capacity to become a two-way method of producing information on demand, transferring electronic mail and engaging in transactional activities, such as teleshopping and telebanking. However, as Jonathan Chevreau of *The Globe and Mail* has written, "two-way videotex versions are faced with the problem that to transmit one needs a two-way cable network, rare in North America, or a telephone system, which is relatively slow and expensive."[69] All of the potential two-way services discussed in this chapter could in fact be delivered using videotex technology via cable systems.

The leading experiment in Canada using Telidon-based technology was Bell Canada's series of Vista experiments, which used a telephone and a television set rather than a cable network. Vista placed 491 user terminals in homes and public places in Toronto, Montreal and Quebec City. It offered information retrieval and teleshopping from 130 organizations. Bell took the position that it was the carrier and not the controller or owner of data being transmitted over the Vista system, an argument that does not eliminate the need to protect personal information. Infomart, a joint effort of the Southam Newspaper Group and *The Toronto Star* (Torstar Inc.), was subcontracted to manage the trial. Infomart prepared, stored and managed information in the Vista system on behalf of other information providers, but was unable to keep the experiment alive, when Bell ended its participation in the fall of 1983.[70]

Infomart continues to manage the Grassroots commercial Telidon service in western Canada. It is also engaged in Videotex America in conjunction with the Times Mirror Co. of Los Angeles. Their Gateway system offers such transactional services as teleshopping, home banking and bill paying, reservations and electronic mail. The Orange County, CA service was to be offered on a commercial basis in September 1984, and was expected to include home shopping and banking, and information retrieval. Infomart had planned to introduce a consumer videotex service the same year in Toronto, using either telephone or cable delivery systems, but by early 1984 it had no immediate plans for home services in Canada.[71]

By the end of 1983, the initiative in developing home videotex services on a commercial basis had shifted from Canada to the U.S., where at least 80 trials and services were in progress using cable, telephone and other transmission mediums. It is reported that 51 organizations in the U.S. are currently developing consumer and business videotex. In February 1984 CBS Inc., IBM and Sears Roebuck and Co. announced a joint venture to provide home videotex services on a commercial basis. AT&T is also actively involved in this area, especially by promoting a low-cost home terminal.[72]

Potential Privacy Problems and Possible Solutions

Some practices for the protection of confidentiality obviously have to be in place for the various types of information-delivery systems employing Telidon-like technology. Videotex, for example, makes possible an exact record of each item withdrawn from a particular information bank. If users are to be charged for a particular piece of information, records identifying users have to be maintained for billing purposes. The software for the various Telidon experiments conducted in recent years is designed in such a way that data on individual usage are produced. The operators can tell what pages individuals have accessed and which persons have done so. A recent Canadian videotex study described consumers' fears about the protection of their privacy and advocated government regulation to "ensure adequate controls over the use of information" and to prevent data base operators from disclosing "behavioral patterns of an individual."[73]

In its Vista experiment, Bell Canada attempted to extend its general policies on confidentiality to the information retrieval and service systems. The experiment helped to identify the various problems that exist for privacy and confidentiality. One is third-party access to billing records, although no billing system for individuals was designed during the experimental stage. Another is the problem of access and use of subscriber lists, which is especially important if electronic mail turns videotex into a mailbox. How long should usage and billing records be maintained? How should message storing and forwarding be handled, especially when personal information is involved? Should data be stored on the videotex system in such a way that user profiles can be compiled? Finally, there are the usual problems of insuring the security of personal information.

In the Vista field trials, Bell Canada entered into contractual agreements with its information providers and the individual participants. It was responsible "for the maintenance and operation of the data base." The general regulations of federally regulated telephone companies applied to the services, equipment and facilities used by the information provider in connection with the field trial, but these do not mention confidentiality. Section 19 of Bell's agreement with the information provider determined that all of the information provided by one party to the other "which is identified as confidential" shall be "held and used in confidence," disclosed only to those employees or agents with the need to know, and used only in connection with "performing any function, conducting any study or taking any action under, or by reason of, or in connection with this agreement."

Bell Canada's Vista agreement with individual participants had the following provision on confidentiality: "Bell agrees that any information it obtains regarding the Participant's use of or attitude towards a Vista Field Trial or Vista Trial Service will be held in confidence and not divulged to others."[74] Presumably this contractual obligation establishes the right of the participant to sue Bell Canada for breach of contract if personal information is disclosed to a third party. Obtaining real satisfaction in the courts for damages suffered is another matter, as there is also a clause in the Vista agreement which seeks to exempt Bell Canada from any liability.

Thus, although no definitive solutions were arrived at, the various Telidon experiments in Canada were conducted with some awareness of the potential problems for personal privacy. A study prepared by the Department of Communications in July 1980 recognized that:

> *Privacy will be a critical issue with the new media.* When large amounts of information on individuals or on individual behavior can be easily and inexpensively accessed in centralized computer-readable media, privacy problems will arise. . . .with new home information services, everything that individuals do while using the service can be monitored and recorded. This information has economic, social and political value. It can be used to the detriment of individuals and can be bought and sold for a fee. It can be used for marketing purposes in valuable ways. Privacy regulations can be envisioned when new services in the home are developed, but the invisible nature of information will make privacy difficult and expensive to achieve. Without it, however, individuals may be deterred from using the new media.[75]

Despite this comprehensive identification of privacy risks, the Department of Communications has not done any significant internal planning on the issue of privacy, except for supporting a seminar in Vancouver in 1981 run by Group West, entitled *Privacy in Videotex.* The Canadian Videotex Consultative Committee, which began work in the fall of 1979, is concerned about the issue of privacy and videotex and in fact initiated the Group West workshop. In a report to the federal Department of Communications in April 1983, the Committee recommended the creation of a Videotex Commission as a mechanism to achieve a national policy to deal with new information technologies.[76]

The solution to privacy problems in videotex lies in the direction provided by the "Model Privacy Guidelines for Videotex Systems," which were published in June 1983 by the Fair Information Practices Committee of the Videotex Industry Association in the United States; these are discussed in Chapter 5.

SUMMARY

In reviewing the discussion in this chapter of the various interactive services—pay-per-view, security services, public opinion-polling, tele-education, teleshopping, telebanking, information retrieval and videotex—it may have occurred to the astute reader that while each type of two-way service opens up a distinct set of risks to consumer privacy, some services are potentially more harmful to privacy than others. It seems evident that information derived in the course of providing security services—for example, the consistent inability (referred to earlier) of a given consumer to enter the proper security code which allows him to gain access to his premises—may lead to greater violations of privacy than might occur from consumer use of a pay-per-view service, in which the most data that could be made available to an outsider were that a given household chose a certain type of program. Yet, in each case, the disclosure of such data would represent the violation of an individual's right to conduct his or her life as he or she chooses, free from external surveillance or interference. In addition, as we have stated previously, information that is considered personal by one individual may not be by another. The significant point is that every one of the interactive services described in this chapter poses a threat to individual privacy, unless policies are formulated and regulations devised which will maximize the chances for maintaining confidentiality of data gathered in the course of providing such a service and minimize the chance for third-party access to, and use of, information that the individual subscriber considers as personal and private.

NOTES

1. Deanna Collingwood Nash and John B. Smith, *Interactive Home Media and Privacy*. Prepared for the Office of Policy Planning, U.S. Federal Trade Commission (Washington, DC: Collingwood Associates, Inc., January 1981), pp. 38–41.

2. *Ibid.*, pp. 41–42.

3. Canadian Radio-television and Telecommunications Commission, "Public Hearings on Non-programming Services," Vancouver, April 28–30, 1981, p. 364. (Hereafter cited as CRTC, *Hearings.*) CRTC, *Hearings,* Toronto, March 10–12, 1981, p. 294.

4. Rogers Cablesystems Inc., *1982 Annual Report* (Toronto, 1983), pp. 12, 17.

5. *Western Ontario Business,* VII, No. 21 (September 27, 1982), p. 8. The London system is now being built.

6. I am indebted to Professor Eric Manning, Director of the Institute for Computer Research at the University of Waterloo, for guidance on these points.

7. Interview, E. Manning.

8. John Wicklein, *Electronic Nightmare: The New Communications and Freedom* (New York: The Viking Press, 1979), p. 181.

9. See Robert Lindsey, "Home Box Office Moves in on Hollywood," *The New York Times Magazine,* June 12, 1983, pp. 31–38, 66–71; Rogers Cable-systems Inc. *1983 Annual Report* (Toronto, 1984), p. 29.

10. Francis Spiller Associates, *New Broadcasting and Communications Services (A Perspective)* (Nepean, Ontario: Francis Spiller Associates, September 1980), pp. 18–20. (Hereafter cited as Spiller, *New Broadcasting and Communications Services.*)

11. *The New York Times,* September 29, 1982, p. C21; Tony Schwartz, "Plan to Present Musical Raises Pay-TV Issues," *The New York Times,* October 30, 1982, p. 14; and Dan Westell, "Broadcasters Voice Skepticism," *The Globe and Mail,* April 8, 1983, p. B15.

12. Cable Telecommunications Research Institute, *Interaction,* IV (December 1983), pp. 7–8.

13. Nash and Smith, *Interactive Home Media and Privacy,* p. 54.

14. Alan F. Westin, "Home Information Systems: The Privacy Debate," *Datamation,* XXVIII, No. 7 (July 1982), p. 104; see also Nash and Smith, *Interactive Home Media and Privacy,* pp. 55–57 for the actual newspaper clippings on the case.

15. Nash and Smith, *Interactive Home Media and Privacy,* pp. 44, 47. See also Sally Bedell Smith, "Battle Intensifying over Explicit Sex on Cable TV," *The New York Times,* Oct. 3, 1983, pp. A1, C22.

16. Presentation by Jeff Campbell, Bell Canada, to the National Secretaries' Association and the Business and Professional Women's Association, March 24, 1981, p. 2.

17. Sylvane Walters, "Two-way CATV Systems," in W. Kaiser, H. Marko and E. Witte, eds., *Two-way Television: Experiences with Pilot Projects in North America, Japan, and Europe.* Proceedings of a Symposium held in Munich, April 27–29, 1977 (Berlin, Heidelberg and New York: Springer Verlag, 1977), pp. 96–97.

18. Wicklein, *Electronic Nightmare,* p. 22.

19. Robert Ellis Smith, "One Perspective on Warner Amex Cable," *Privacy Journal,* IX (February 1983), p. 3; *Marketing News,* May 2, 1980, p. 6.

20. Nash and Smith, *Interactive Home Media and Privacy,* p. 52.

21. *Privacy Times,* II, No. 1 (January 19, 1982), p. 3.

22. *Privacy Journal,* X (June, 1984), p. 1.

23. Nash and Smith, *Interactive Home Media and Privacy,* p. 8.

24. Edmund Rapaport, "Are Statisticians Entitled To Use Administrative Records?" International Statistical Institute, Buenos Aires, Argentina, December, 1981, pp. 3–4. For further discussion, see David H. Flaherty, *Privacy and Government Data Banks. An International Perspective* (London, U.K.: Mansell, 1979), passim.

25. Manitoba, Department of Consumer, Corporate and Internal Services, Communications and Information Services Division, *Broadcasting and Cable Television: A Manitoba Perspective. Discussion Paper* (Winnipeg: Government of Manitoba, 1974), p. 14.

26. *The New York Times,* September 29, 1982, p. C21. See also *Time,* September 12, 1983, pp. 58–59.

27. *Warner Amex News,* VI, Nos. 10/11 (October/November 1982), p. 2; John Andrew, "Home Security Is a Cable TV, Industry Bets," *The Wall Street Journal,* September 15, 1981; *Time,* November 21, 1983, p. 104. Warner Amex's main competition comes from security equipment sold to other cable operators by Tocom Inc. of Dallas and from AT&T Consumer Products, which offers a fire-alert system linking smoke alarms to phones that will dial two numbers when smoke is detected.

28. See the system's description in CRTC, *Hearings,* Vancouver, April 28–30, 1981, pp. 277, 284–285; Canadian Radio-television and Telecommunications Commission, *Decisions CRTC 81-919 to CRTC 81-922,* Ottawa, December 30, 1981.

29. Rogers Cablesystems Inc., *1981 Annual Report,* p. 22; Rogers Cablesystems Inc., *1982 Annual Report,* pp. 10–11, 24.

30. Bell Canada, "Public Attitudes Toward the Micro-Electronic Technologies" (May 1982), pp. 6–8.

31. Charles D. Elliott, *Cable Security Services. A First-Hand Report* (Research Report, Cable Telecommunications Research Institute, Ottawa, January 1982). The initial cost of cable-based security is a major obstacle to the growth of the market. Ottawa Cablevision estimates that it costs a home-owner $1100 on average to install Cableguard (Cable Telecommunications Research Institute, *Interaction,* III, No. 3 [December 1982] p. 8).

32. See *Personal Privacy in an Information Society. The Report of the Privacy Protection Study Commission* (Washington, DC, 1977), pp. 52–55.

33. CRTC, *Introductory Statement Relating to Decisions CRTC 81-919 to CRTC 81-922. Applications for the Cable Distribution of Non-Programming Services on an Experimental Basis.* (Ottawa: Canadian Radio-television and Telecommunications Commission, December 30, 1981.) (Hereafter cited as CRTC, *Introductory Statement.*).

34. CRTC, *Hearings*, Vancouver, April 28-30, 1981, p. 321.

35. Nash and Smith, *Interactive Home Media and Privacy*, p. 36; Wicklein, *Electronic Nightmare*, p. 18; Sally Bedell, "Two-Way Cable TV Network Starts," *The New York Times*, May 2, 1983, p. C20; *The Boston Globe*, January 20, 1984, p. 20. QUBE in Pittsburgh also offers opinion-polling and pay-per-view services.

36. *Western Ontario Business*, VII, No. 21 (September 27, 1982), p. 8. Rogers' opinion-polling service in Portland can simply be used for multiple choice questions.

37. CRTC, *Introductory Statement*, December 30, 1981, pp. 6-7. The specific requirements were incorporated in CRTC Decision 81-920, which allowed a series of Rogers cable companies to offer public opinion-polling services.

38. See CRTC, *Hearings*, Toronto, March 10-12, 1981, pp. 209, 313; CRTC, *Hearings*, Vancouver, April 28-30, 1981, p. 370.

39. CRTC, *Hearings*, Vancouver, April 28-30, 1981, p. 370.

40. See the discussion in Flaherty, *Privacy and Government Data Banks*, pp. 212-226.

41. Wicklein, *Electronic Nightmare*, pp. 25-26.

42. Nash and Smith, *Interactive Home Media and Privacy*, p. 54. For a wide-ranging discussion of the impact of two-way polling, especially in the QUBE system, see David Burnham, *The Rise of the Computer State* (New York: Random House, 1983), pp. 241-250.

43. Nash and Smith, *Interactive Home Media and Privacy*, p. 43.

44. *Le Groupe Videotron* (Montreal, April 27, 1982), p. 17; CRTC, *Decision 81-919*, p. 2.

45. TV Ontario, *C and U News*, II, No. 2 (May 1982), pp. 4-5; *Western News* (University of Western Ontario), March 11, 1982, p. 3.

46. I have not discussed the service known as "play" cable, whereby a company offers electronic games to subscribers on a one-way basis, since its implications for privacy are so minimal.

47. CRTC, *Introductory Statement,* December 30, 1981, p. 5; CRTC, *Hearings,* Toronto, March 10–12, 1981, p. 297. See Dan Fesperman, "Will Shopping Malls Disappear?", *Toronto Sunday Star,* July 31, 1983, p. H2.

48. Spiller, *New Broadcasting and Communications Services,* pp. 29–31; *The Sunday Times,* October 10, 1982, Business News, p. 1; *The Economist,* 282, No. 7227 (March 6, 1982), pp. 11, 25.

49. CRTC, *Decision 81-919,* December 30, 1981; CRTC, *Decision 81-290,* December 30, 1981; CRTC, *Hearings,* Toronto, March 10–12, 1981, pp. 210–211, 278; CRTC, *Hearings,* Vancouver, April 28–30, 1981, p. 290.

50. *The Globe and Mail,* September 1, 1982, p. B5; *Computing Canada,* VIII (April 15, 1982), p. 4.

51. See Lawrence Moule, "Consumers Sign on for TV Shopping Experiment," *The Toronto Star,* July 18, 1982, p. H2.

52. This paragraph is based on *The Cable Television Advertising Market 1982-87* (White Plains, Knowledge Industry Publications, Inc., 1982), pp. 51-57.

53. Sidney L. Gardner and Robin White, *New Technology and the Right to Privacy: State Responses to Federal Inaction. A Report to the New York State Consumer Protection Board.* (Unpublished draft, August 1982), p. 37.

54. *ABA Banking Journal,* February 1982, pp. 96–101; Alan F. Westin, "Home Information Systems: The Privacy Debate," *Datamation,* XXVIII, No. 7 (July 1982), p. 100. See also Robert Steklasa, "Dial-a-bank with a TV Set Gets Closer," *The Financial Post,* October 2, 1982, p. 1.

55. See "Teletext and Videotex," *Broadcasting,* June 28, 1982, p. 49; Dennis Slocum, "Efficiency Strong Spur Toward Cashless Society," *The Globe and Mail,* November 2, 1982, p. B1; Joanne Strong, "The Informal John Kelly," *The Globe and Mail,* April 9, 1983, p. 20; David Stewart-Patterson, "Nabu, Industry Analysts are Divided on Future of Cable Computer Service," *The Globe and Mail,* July 25, 1983, p. B1. Nabu is a major promoter of two-way services over cable systems.

56. *The Globe and Mail,* November 18, 1983, p. B13.

57. *The Boston Globe,* June 19, 1984, p. 37.

58. See the discussion in David H. Flaherty, *Privacy, Confidentiality and Security in a Canadian Electronic Funds Transfer System.* Ontario Electronic Funds Transfer Study Project, Working Paper No. 5 (Toronto: Ministry of the Attorney General, 1978).

59. See Alan F. Westin, "Privacy Issues and the Implications of In-Home Banking," *American Banker,* June 3, 1981; and Lorena Kern Davitt, "The Right to Financial Privacy Act: New Protection for Financial Records," *Fordham Urban Law Journal,* VIII (1979-1980), pp. 597-627.

60. Bank of Montreal, *Your Privacy, How the Bank of Montreal Protects It* (Montreal, 1982); and Bank of Montreal, *166th Annual Report 1983* (Montreal, 1984) p. 40. There are considerable difficulties in ensuring that such lofty principles are observed in practice, especially at the branch bank level.

61. CRTC, *Decision 81-919,* December 30, 1981, p. 3; CRTC, *Hearings,* Vancouver, April 28-30, 1981, p. 412.

62. *Cable Communications Magazine,* XLVIII, No. 8 (August 1982), pp. 13-14.

63. Spiller, *New Broadcasting and Communications Services,* p. 17.

64. See *Computerworld,* XVI (May 3, 1982), pp. 2-3; *Time,* July 26, 1982.

65. Grant Buckler, "Cable Seen as a Data Medium," *Computing Canada,* October 14, 1982, p. 42.

66. See Jonathan Chevreau, "Ottawa Cable TV Firm to Offer Software by Wire," *The Globe and Mail,* June 4, 1982, p. B6; *The Globe and Mail,* June 3, 1982, p. B3; and Cable Telecommunications Research Institute, *Interaction,* IV (December 1983), p. 6.

67. See David Thomas, *Knights of the New Technology* (Toronto: Key Porter, 1983), pp. 71-80; *The Globe and Mail,* January 27, 1984, pp. B15, B20; *The Globe and Mail,* April 27, 1984, p. B13; *The Globe and Mail,* June 19, 1984, p. B8; and *The London Free Press,* June 14, 1984, p. A9.

68. See Charles Dalfen, *An Industry in Transition. Regulatory Aspects of the New Technology.* Royal Commission on Newspapers Research Reports, April 6, 1981, Appendix A, Appendix B and pp. 44-45. A recent Canadian videotex study, which is very positive about the prospects for teleshopping, is Stephen B. Ash and John A. Quelch, *The New Video Technology and its Impact on Retailers in Canada.* Research Report, Technological Innovation Studies Program. (Ottawa: Department of Industry, Trade and Commerce,

November 1982). See also Barry Lesser, *Alternative Market Structure for Videotex Service in Canada: The Public Policy Implications* (Center for Development Projects, Dalhousie University for Ottawa: Department of Communications, revised July 1982); Phil Hirsch, "Future of Videotex/Teletext Remains Uncertain," *Computerworld*, XVII (April 25, 1983), p. 21; Hirsch, "Videotex/Teletext Assailed for Promises," *Computerworld*, XVII (May 9, 1983), pp. 63–64; and "Mass Markets for Teletext and Videotex Expected to Emerge in 1987," *Information Hotline*, XV (May 1983), p. 1.

69. *Computing Canada*, April 29, 1982, p. 12; *The Globe and Mail*, June 26, 1982, p. B1.

70. Dalfen, *Industry in Transition*, pp. 33–34; Spiller, *New Broadcasting and Communications Services*, pp. 35–37; *The Globe and Mail*, September 9, 1983, p. B11.

71. *Computing Canada*, February 4, 1982, pp. 1, 11; *The Globe and Mail*, April 22, 1983, p. B13; and Jonathan Chevreau, "Infomart Planning Inexpensive Service," *The Globe and Mail*, February 9, 1983, "Report on Business;" *The Globe and Mail*, February 10, 1984, p. B13; *The Globe and Mail*, July 27, 1984, p. T1; and Thomas, *Knights of the New Technology*, pp. 135–139.

72. *The Globe and Mail*, February 10, 1984, p. B13; *The Globe and Mail*, February 16, 1984, p. B17; *The Globe and Mail*, June 20, 1984, p. B13; and *The Globe and Mail*, July 20, 1984, p. B13.

73. Ash and Quelch, *The New Video Technology and its Impact on Retailers in Canada*, pp. 65, 72, 119–120.

74. Agreement Between the Participant and Bell Canada, 1981, Section 9.

75. Morris Estabrooks, *Videotex. An Economic and Policy Assessment* (Ottawa: Department of Communications, Communications Economics Branch, July 1980), p. 40.

76. *Computing Canada*, IX (April 14, 1983), p. 7.

5

Regulatory Initiatives in the U.S.

Since two-way cable television and telephone services pose clear challenges to the protection of personal privacy, the next three chapters review some of the attempts being made to solve these real and potential problems. The development of solutions is more advanced in the United States than in Canada, particularly in the field of "cable privacy," and is examined in this chapter. Chapter 6 is a brief survey of international efforts at promoting data protection. Chapter 7 reviews the various federal and provincial regulatory options in Canada and then evaluates the process of self-regulation by the cable industry as a means of resolving the problems of privacy posed by interactive services.

MUNICIPAL ORDINANCES AND FRANCHISE CONTRACTS

In most of the American states, individual municipalities handle the franchising of cable television systems. A number of these communities have developed local ordinances and franchising contracts with cable companies in order to deal with questions of privacy, confidentiality and security. Municipalities such as Evanston, IL, Detroit, Tucson and Lakewood, CA impose prohibitions on the use of subscriber information through stipulations in franchise agreements with cable companies or as part of city ordinances. The franchise ordinances and contracts entered into by Rogers Cablesystems and Maclean Hunter in the United States exemplify the kinds of protective measures that should accompany all two-way services.

Rogers has franchise contracts affecting its cable television operations in Syracuse, NY, Portland, OR and the suburbs of Minneapolis. Section 16.4 of the Syracuse contract lays down regulations concerning subscriber privacy in the operation of security services, currently the only available two-way system:

a) Except as required to provide a service authorized by this agreement, including but not limited to the alarm system, the Company, the City, or any other person shall neither initiate nor use any procedure or device for procuring information or data from a subscriber's terminals by any means, without the prior valid authorization of the affected subscriber. Valid authorization shall mean written approval from the subscriber which shall not have been obtained from the subscriber as a condition of service and which may be revoked by the subscriber at any time.

b) Except as required to provide a service authorized by this agreement, including but not limited to the alarm system, the City, the Company or any other person shall not, without prior written authorization of the affected subscriber, provide data identifying or designating any subscriber. Any data authorized shall be made available to the authorizing subscriber in understandable fashion.

In addition, Section 16.5 of the Syracuse contract prohibits the tapping or monitoring of the cable system for any purpose whatsoever without the authorization of the subscriber.[1]

Section 9 of the cable ordinance that regulates Rogers' operations in the suburbs of Minneapolis provides a somewhat complicated procedure for informed consent:

A. . . .Grantee [the cable company] and any other person shall neither initiate nor use any procedure or device for procuring or storing information or data from a subscriber's terminals or terminal by any means, without the prior authorization of the affected subscriber which shall not have been obtained from the subscriber as a condition of service. The request for such authorization shall be contained in a separate document and identify the purpose for which the data or information is being gathered or stored. After the first year of the authorization's initial signing, Grantee shall, for each year said authorization is in effect without revocation, mail a notice to each authorizing subscriber informing him or her of his right to revoke said authorization. The authorization shall be revocable at any time by the subscriber without penalty of any kind whatsoever. A separate authorization shall be required for each type or classification of data or information sought from a subscriber terminal.

B. Grantee shall not, without the written authorization of the affected subscriber, provide to anyone data identifying or designating any subscriber. Any data authorized shall be made available upon request by and without charge to the authorizing subscriber in understandable fashion, including specification of the purpose for which the information is being gathered and to whom and for what fee the information is to be sold.

The Rogers Minneapolis ordinance seems to be the strictest of the several agreements discussed here, but the point is that all of them offer strong protection for the privacy of consumers using two-way services.

In various American franchise applications Maclean Hunter subsidiaries have undertaken to protect the privacy of subscribers in accordance with the requirements of local franchise ordinances. In its application for the Milwaukee franchise (which it did not obtain), Maclean Hunter agreed to comply with Section 99.10(5) of the local ordinance concerning the protection of the rights of individuals. The ordinance includes the need for the express written permission of the subscriber, valid for only one year, before information could be collected on "individual viewing patterns or practices. . . ." Written authorization is required for each type or classification of information collected from subscribers. The Milwaukee ordinance further prohibits the disclosure of subscriber information: "Any information concerning individual subscriber viewing habits or responses, except for information for billing purposes, shall be destroyed within sixty (60) days. Information for billing purposes shall be kept for two (2) years and then destroyed unless otherwise required to be kept by law." The same ordinance also prohibits (without written authorization) the sale or dissemination of the names and addresses of subscribers or any lists which identify the viewing habits of individual subscribers.

Canadian cable companies like to do business in the U.S. for a variety of reasons, one of which is the less regulated business environment thought to prevail there. Yet both Rogers and Maclean Hunter have agreed to comply with fairly strong provisions to protect subscriber privacy as a condition of doing business. Thus, it should be simple enough to voluntarily extend similar protections to Canadian cable subscribers as two-way services are introduced. If self-regulation is not forthcoming in due course, the Canadian Radio-television and Telecommunications Commission (CRTC) in particular must imitate American municipalities by including appropriate provisions in its licensing decisions for the protection of privacy in non-programming services.

PRIVACY CODES

In addition to Warner Amex's exemplary Code of Privacy, a number of state cable television associations have begun to adopt privacy codes to be followed by all member cable operators. The Videotex Industry Association of the United States has also issued a set of guidelines to help its members deal with privacy problems. These various self-regulatory efforts are discussed below.

The Warner Amex Code of Privacy

Warner Amex Cable Communications Inc. issued its code of privacy in October 1981. This 500-word document (see Appendix A for full text of code) furnishes an admirable example of voluntary self-regulation of a new information technology. In an introductory statement, Gustave M. Hauser, then chairman of the company, stated that the code is "an effective, workable set of standards, procedures and policies respecting subscriber privacy," developed in the course of implementing the QUBE service.

The code has 11 specific provisions that incorporate the traditional principles of a code of fair information practices, as contained in most data protection laws. Warner Amex agrees to keep subscribers informed of the information-gathering functions of the interactive services being provided and to keep subscriber information physically secure and confidential. Agreements with subscribers specify the terms under which information will be used, primarily for billing and implementation of all subscriber services. No other individualized information concerning viewing or responses will be developed "unless the subscriber has been advised in advance and given adequate opportunity not to participate." However, Warner Amex does use the information collected to develop statistical and non-identifiable data, which could have negative implications for individual and group privacy, especially in cases where only one neighborhood in a particular community is served by an interactive system.[2]

Despite the admirable assurances of the Warner Amex code, a subscriber should keep in mind the intrinsic risks to privacy inherent in the use of any two-way system. For example, in Article 5 the company promises to refuse requests to make any individual subscriber information available to government agencies in the absence of legal compulsion, such as a court order or a subpoena. If such requests occur, Warner Amex "will promptly notify the subscriber prior to responding if permitted to do so by law." On a more positive note, subscribers may have access to the information collected about them, which will only be retained so long as is reasonably necessary; they also can have their names removed from mailing lists developed by Warner Amex and its associated companies.

One of the consultants on the preparation of the Warner Amex code, Ronald L. Plesser, has made the important point that although the code is voluntary in its inception, it is self-enforcing: "it is being made a part of all subscriber contracts and franchise agreements. As a result, compliance becomes more than merely voluntary. Of course, the Code in itself cannot defend against governmental access other than through its insistence upon legal process. That part of the issue may require examination if and when problems do develop."[3]

The Warner Amex August 1982 franchise application for Tucson, Arizona illustrates the company's commitment to the protection of personal privacy. It specifically notes the extent to which the individual subscriber agreement incorporates the basic provisions of the Warner Amex privacy code. The application concludes "that the public is, and is likely to remain, deeply concerned about privacy, and we [Warner Amex] commit to reviewing and updating our privacy policy on a yearly basis to keep abreast of consumer concerns."

Other Voluntary Codes of Privacy

In May 1982 the New York State Cable Television Association became the first state association in the U.S. to adopt a privacy code for all its member cable systems. (The inspiration may have come from the efforts of state Attorney General Robert Abrams to legislate for cable privacy, as discussed in the next section of this chapter.) One basic premise for voluntary action in New York State has direct relevance to the situation everywhere: "Although the actual widespread implementation of home information services will not occur until sometime in the future, we believe that now is the time for the cable television industry to address the questions and take appropriate action to ensure against any potential invasion of subscriber privacy." The association further established a committee to meet four times a year "to review the Code in light of new developments, and to make such changes as are necessary or desirable to provide all reasonable protections for the privacy of their subscribers."

The privacy code of the New York State Cable Television Association is virtually identical to the Warner Amex code. The only difference is found in Article 5, which seems to be somewhat stronger than Article 3 of the Warner Amex code, and reads as follows:

> 5. Neither Cable Company nor any other party authorized by Cable Company shall monitor, gather, or utilize the information derived from any individual subscriber's connection for any purpose whatsoever without the prior written authorization of each affected subscriber provided, however, that Cable Company nevertheless may conduct system-wide or individual addressed 'sweeps' for the purpose of verifying system integrity, for billing purposes or for providing a requested service.

Both the New England Cable Television Association, Inc. and the New Jersey Cable Television Association have subsequently adopted codes of privacy. The former is virtually identical with the Warner Amex privacy code, and a number of cable operators have already subscribed to it. The code produced by the New Jersey Cable Television Association is also essentially the same as the Warner Amex code, except that Article 5 of the New Jersey version is the same as the New York code quoted in the previous paragraph. In addition, Article 7 of the New Jersey document specifies that subscribers may examine and copy all billing information pertaining to them, rather than allowing subscribers access to all information developed by the cable company.

In June 1983 the Videotex Industry Association of the United States released its "Model Privacy Guidelines for Videotex Systems."[4] This document represents an initial effort on the part of an association with more than 120 member firms to address potential privacy problems. The guidelines permit a system operator to collect and use individually identifiable information for five reasons: 1) to provide a service requested by a consumer; 2) to maintain technical operations; 3) to prevent unauthorized use of a system; 4) to bill customers; and 5) to conduct market research in order to compile bulk information that will not identify individual customers. Any other uses or disclosures of individual information require the consent of the subscriber or a compulsory legal order. The guidelines further require the system operator to "make all reasonable efforts to safeguard individual information against unauthorized access." Also, system operators are to encourage service providers on videotex systems, such as banks and retailers, to comply with the guidelines. Finally, "individual information will be retained only as long as it is needed for the purposes for which it was collected."

Although the Videotex Industry Association encourages videotex operators to follow the guidelines, they are not binding on the industry, and some companies may alter some of the specifics. CompuServe and Viewdata Corp. of America have adopted their own privacy codes based on the guidelines.

Are Voluntary Codes Adequate?

Alan Westin has stated that the Warner Amex privacy code "represents a well-formulated and responsible voluntary action by a service provider, comparable to the employee privacy policies that IBM and a few other progressive companies pioneered in the early 1970s." He has also effectively summarized the criticisms that can be advanced against such voluntary codes:

> There has been some concern that not all operators will adopt these rules, especially where they threaten to diminish income from secondary uses of subscriber data. There is also concern that the company codes do not provide for penalties to punish employee violations or proper damages to subscribers who might be harmed. It has also been stressed that no voluntary code can cope with the demands for information that government or third parties might make through legal process.[5]

Attorney General Abrams has made similar points publicly and vigorously. In testimony before a committee of the New York Assembly in May 1982 he cited the "strong economic motivation to use and sell personal subscriber information," which would not be adequately counteracted by self-regulation.[6]

A study by Sidney Gardner and Robin White for the New York State Consumer Protection Board brought to light yet further problems involved in enforcing voluntary codes of privacy: "At the most basic level, we are troubled by the ultimate unenforceability of voluntary codes. . . .such codes may only last as long as the firm's current management. Moreover, voluntary codes provide dissatisfied customers with no avenues of recourse when they believe their privacy has been infringed. Even given the best of management intentions, one cannot predict future uses and abuses of records containing sensitive personal data."[7] A partial response to such criticisms is that Warner Amex in particular is making its privacy code part of specific contractual agreements with individual subscribers, but such agreements nevertheless remain difficult to enforce.

Robert Ellis Smith, the editor of the Washington-based *Privacy Journal,* is especially critical of relying on the Warner Amex privacy code. He notes that it is voluntary and may be revoked at any time by the company, which may also interpret the code as it wishes. Smith is concerned that the grouping of subscriber data could lead to information being refined on very small groups of individuals living in specific census blocks or zip-code areas. One of his most persuasive points is that current legislation does not prevent Warner Amex "from releasing individual or bulk subscriber information to its many corporate affiliates." Finally, Smith is concerned about the possibility of Warner Amex offering a discount to any subscriber willing to give a blanket waiver to the clause on nondisclosure of information; one could plausibly argue in favor of the right of individuals to put a monetary value on reducing the level of personal privacy they enjoy.[8]

Another significant criticism of the private sector comes from Professor David Linowes, former chairman of the U.S. Privacy Protection Study Commission, who notes that companies have generally failed to respond adequately to the Commission's 1977 recommendations that they should adopt basic fair information practices.[9] Although the Commission and President Jimmy Carter accepted the notion of giving businesses time to self-regulate, the lack of results suggests the necessity of new statutory initiatives.

Some further doubts about the adequacy of self-regulation, despite the actions of Warner Amex, the New York State Cable Television Association and similar organizations, derive from the fact that Warner Amex is the only firm out of the 2000 members of the National Cable Television Association that has produced or adopted a voluntary privacy policy. In an editorial on February 8, 1982, *CableVision* described privacy codes as "good for all. . .we are confident that Warner's code is but the first of many such codes that operators will develop. In time, we are also sure that the NCTA will want to join with the operating companies to develop an industry-wide standard."

Later that year, Alan Westin joined the list of those urging the National Cable Television Association (NCTA) to move towards the development of an industry-wide code. He noted that the NCTA had "been content to assert that because there are no fully-operating commercial systems and because no operator abuses have taken place, legislators and regulatory agencies should leave the industry alone."[10] The regulatory situation in fact took a dramatic new turn in 1982 as a number of states either passed cable privacy acts or seriously contemplated such legislation. Moreover, the NCTA itself took at least initial steps towards preparing a national code of cable privacy (which has become primarily an effort to shape federal cable privacy legislation), and other state associations began to imitate the New York State Cable Television Association.

Because of their inability to prevent third party access to identifiable subscriber data—in particular, access on the part of government agencies—privacy codes are not a remedy for all the privacy-related ills stemming from the use of two-way services. Nevertheless, voluntary codes represent an essential step in self-regulation that should be adopted by all companies offering interactive services.

CABLE PRIVACY LEGISLATION

Recent U.S. legislative efforts support the view that two-way services do pose significant risks for personal privacy. Even though such steps have been taken without the enthusiastic support, in some instances, of the cable television industry, the legislatures of such important states as Illinois, Wisconsin, California and Connecticut passed cable privacy statutes between 1981 and 1983. (It should be noted that the four states that passed privacy statutes all had operational interactive cable systems in place by mid-1982. No more than a total of 14 states had any actively operating two-way systems in effect at that time, most of them providing home security services only.) The industry's objections to such legislation are discussed below in the section on a proposed cable privacy bill in New York state. The arguments are, of course, endemic to private sector efforts to avoid privacy regulations.

Illinois: The Communications Consumer Privacy Act

On September 16, 1981 the governor of Illinois signed into law The Communications Consumer Privacy Act, which became effective January 1, 1982. It applies broadly to "any person or organization which owns, controls, operates or manages any company which provides information or entertainment electronically to a household, including but not limited to a cable or community antenna television system." The law is only a page long, yet it prohibits a number of activities:

> Section 3.(a) It shall be unlawful for a communications company to:
> (1) install and use any equipment which would allow a communications company to visually observe or listen to what is occurring in an individual subscriber's household without the knowledge or permission of the subscriber; (2) provide any person or public or private organization with a list containing the name of a subscriber, unless the communications company gives notice thereof to the subscriber; (3) disclose the television viewing habits of any individual subscriber without the subscriber's consent; or (4) install or maintain a home-protection scanning device in a dwelling as part of a communication service without the express written consent of the occupant.

A violation of any provision of Section 3 can lead to a fine not to exceed $10,000 for each infraction. Moreover, "any person who has been injured by a violation of this Section may commence an action in the circuit court for damages against any communications company which has committed a violation. If the court awards damages, the plaintiff shall be awarded costs."[11]

Even though the Illinois statute is relatively simple in comparison to its successors in other states, it takes the important step of providing for punitive penalties for invasions of privacy and applies to any electronic home service. While this legislation represented an early constructive measure to curb privacy violations, in 1983 the American Civil Liberties Union of Illinois promoted a Cable Television Privacy bill on the grounds that the 1981 law was not strong enough. The new bill resembled the other state cable privacy statutes that are discussed below. But the Illinois bill was defeated in the House of Representatives in May 1984. Private industry, led by bankers and retail merchants, headed the opposition. The episode is especially instructive, since it suggests that the strong support for such legislation in states like California may not be duplicated elsewhere and that some significant political battles will have to be fought, unless federal legislation sweeps the field in the interim.

Wisconsin Legislation

The Wisconsin cable privacy statute was passed in the spring of 1982 and became effective on September 26 of that year. The legislature determined "that the use of cable television may infringe on the right of privacy in this state. Therefore, the legislature finds that it is necessary to regulate those aspects of cable television operations that may infringe upon an individual's privacy." The most original provision in the Wisconsin statute determines that an individual subscriber may request the installation of a device that allows him to block the reception and transmission of messages by the cable equipment, except for messages recurring at constant intervals, including those related to security, fire and utility service. The latter qualification was an amendment to the original bill.[12]

Section Two of the Wisconsin statute stipulates that the cable company cannot, "without the written consent of the subscriber given within the preceding 2 years: (a) Monitor the subscriber's cable equipment or the use of it, except to verify the system's integrity or to collect information for billing of pay services," or "(b) Provide anyone with the name or address or other information that discloses or reasonably leads to the disclosure of any aspect of the behavior, including but not limited to individual habits, preferences or finances, of the subscriber or of a member of the subscriber's household." The law provides for criminal penalties in the form of heavy fines for invasions of privacy. An individual is also entitled to the same relief for invasion of privacy as set forth in the state's general right of privacy act, and this may include compensatory damages.

The Wisconsin cable privacy legislation originated with Democratic Representative Marlin Schneider. Aware that cable franchises were being awarded in major Wisconsin cities and that one interactive system was already furnishing a home security service, he determined to formulate "a protective law *before* the technology was all in place." His initial goal was to include basic privacy protections in municipal franchising rules, but the Wisconsin Cable Communications Association said it favored a statewide law, if protections for privacy were to be enacted. Although there was little publicity for the draft legislation, a timely newspaper editorial helped to persuade the legislature, as did the bipartisan support provided by a Republican legislator, whose military intelligence background had familiarized him with the capabilities of surveillance technology.[13]

California Legislation

In August 1982 the California legislature passed a cable privacy statute that became effective on January 1, 1983. Cable industry representatives supported the legislation, which passed through both the Assembly and the Senate on unanimous votes on the main issue.[14] Because California has such a large population and is so influential, this initiative is particularly important.

Assembly Bill 2735 in California, which is approximately three pages in length, amends the California Penal Code to prohibit anyone involved in the ownership or operation of a cable television company from using "any electronic device to record, transmit, or observe any events or listen to, record, or monitor any conversations which take place inside a subscriber's residence, workplace, or place of business, without obtaining the express written consent of the subscriber." The statute also forbids a cable company from providing "any person with any individually identifiable information regarding any of its subscribers, including, but not limited to, the subscriber's television viewing habits, shopping choices, interests, opinions, energy uses, medical information, banking data or information, or any other personal or private information without the subscriber's express written consent." Cable companies may retain and use identifiable subscriber information, including viewing responses, "only to the extent reasonably necessary for billing purposes and internal business practices, and to monitor for unauthorized reception of services." The law also covers "any person receiving subscriber information" from a cable company. The latter may maintain and distribute a list containing only the names and addresses of its subscribers, if they are first offered the option of being excluded from such a list.[15]

Section One of the California statute further contains an important provision on government access to cable information, which reflects the wording of the Warner Amex privacy code:

> c) A cable television corporation shall not make individual subscriber information available to government agencies in the absence of legal compulsion, including, but not limited to, a court order or subpoena. If requests for such information are made, a cable television corporation shall promptly notify the subscriber of the nature of the request and what government agency has requested the information prior to responding unless otherwise prohibited from doing so by law.

The law further provides for criminal penalties in the form of a fine and/or imprisonment for breach of its provisions, and the right to sue for civil damages for invasion of privacy.

Connecticut Legislation

In May 1983 Connecticut became the fourth state to enact cable privacy legislation. Title 16-333(d) of a law on Public Service Companies required the Department of Public Utility to:

> . . .adopt regulations in accordance with chapter 54 (1) establishing personal privacy protections for community antenna television subscribers, including, but not limited to, standards for the types of individually identifiable data that a community antenna television company may collect on its subscribers, (2) requiring each such company to notify each of its subscribers of such privacy protections and (3) prohibiting each such company from disclosing such data without the prior approval of the subscriber.

The legislation directed the Department to adopt such regulations before March 1, 1984 and to incorporate their provisions in each new or existing certificate of public convenience and necessity issued to a cable company.[16] However, as of fall 1984, the regulations had not yet been adopted and were awaiting approval of the state attorney general.

According to a statement made in *The New York Times* by the Attorney General of Connecticut, "the cable companies could soon have more information about individual Americans than anyone—including the Federal Government. . . .We need tough, strict privacy laws governing the collection and dissemination of information gathered by cable TV operators on their subscribers." A subsequent letter to the editor argued that the Connecticut law "does not go far enough in alerting us to the abuse inherent in computer data collection." The writer attacked existing privacy codes on the grounds that "a corporation's primary responsibility is to protect the economic well-being of its shareholders, not the political rights of its customers. When the two conflict, corporations will revise their privacy codes."[17]

New York State: The Controversy Continues

The greatest controversy over cable privacy in the U.S. to date occurred in New York in early 1982, when Attorney General Abrams proposed a state cable privacy bill. Although the bill has not yet been enacted into law, it has generated a great deal of debate. Whereas the enactments in other states, discussed above, are brief, the proposed Cable Privacy Act of 1982 in New York was 22 pages long.

It should be noted that although the first example of a two-way system in New York, either in operation or under construction, was the security system operated by Rogers in Syracuse, the bill received a great deal of press and radio attention throughout the state. *The New York Times* and leading New York City television stations produced editorials in general support of the proposal.[18]

In April and May 1982 the New York State Assembly's standing committee on governmental operations held hearings on the topic of "The Future of Cable Television in New York State." On May 6 Attorney General Abrams testified that "no one disputes the fact that cable companies will become the repository of the most detailed and intimate personal profile of our citizens yet imagined. None of the industry representatives who have testified, or will testify, can dispute that unauthorized disclosure of this detailed personal information would constitute a serious violation of the subscriber's privacy." Abrams also responded to the industry's argument that statutory protection should only be enacted when self-regulation had failed: "the short answer to this argument must be that if the industry is truly serious about privacy protection, it should not oppose enshrining the principle in law, and it would welcome the strong deterrent that this law will erect. In fact, this bill would enhance the industry's ability to enforce its voluntary code or other internal enforcement measures." The Attorney General's discussion is particularly significant, since most companies offering interactive services will no doubt advance the same arguments against detailed regulation at the present time.

Abrams emphasized "that cable companies have strong economic motivation to store and sell personal data. . . the information transmitted to cable companies will be far more detailed, and therefore more valuable, than the type of data previously available." He also argued that the recent quantum leaps in storage capacity of computers actually make it cheaper to retain than to destroy information: "protecting privacy, in other words, may cost the cable companies money, which further casts doubt on the wisdom of acceding to self-regulation." (As noted in Chapter 4, his conclusions on storage are debatable.) Abrams' second major argument against self-regulation, and a crucial one, is "the lack of meaningful sanctions, deterrents, and compensation for victims." In addition, he points out, the proposed cable privacy act restricts the company's property rights in this information and grants the subscriber certain rights concerning the uses to which it may be put. Finally, the New York bill seeks to control disclosures to governmental authorities.

In essence, Abrams put forth a compelling argument that "we must build safeguards into the system rather than be faced with the much more costly and complicated process of cleaning up a mess already created, and the impossible task of reconstructing damaged lives."

No doubt in part as a response to the Abrams' initiative, the State of New York Commission on Cable Television announced on March 3, 1983 that it intended to establish rules and regulations concerning subscriber privacy. This decision was a product of a one-year inquiry into the subject by the commission. It acknowledged that "when subscribers use interactive cable TV, they often convey confidential information concerning themselves to a centralized computer or computer system. For example, banking services may place the individual's banking records into computer storage; remote medical diagnosis and advice would involve storage of medical records; opinion polling, although it clearly has value in many respects, would necessarily involve the compilation of information which a person might prefer to remain private." The commission recognized "that the time has come to devise a new legal framework to reflect the altered social circumstances that new systems create." With respect to the protection of privacy, it found that "having a one-way, two-way or interactive cable system in his home does expose a subscriber to risk of invasion of his privacy." The three pages of proposed regulations on "Subscriber Privacy" cover such matters as informed consent, the inspection and correction of files, and company practices.[19]

The initiative described in the previous paragraph had an extraordinary aftermath. The commission did publish rules and regulations on cable privacy for public comment. Subsequently the chairman of the commission announced publicly that the process of rulemaking would be discontinued, because such rules were in his view unnecessary and there had been no complaints from the public concerning cable privacy.

Early in 1984 New York State Assemblyman Melvin N. Zimmer, along with 91 cosponsors, introduced a Cable Telecommunications Privacy Bill. The House Government Operations Committee held hearings on Bill 7327a in several cities in the state. The Bill, which contained strong protective provisions similar to those found in other cable privacy laws, was passed unanimously in the Assembly in March and then died in a Senate Committee. Since Bill 7327a was designed as a study bill, both the Assembly and the Senate developed new bills on cable privacy in June 1984. The Senate passed its version with the support of the Direct Mail Marketing Association, but the Assembly did not act and is not expected to do anything further in this election year. The Assembly version is oriented less to cable technology than to the protection of personal information, which is the thrust of the New York State Protection of Personal Privacy in Public Records Act of 1983. Further legislative attention to cable privacy is expected in New York in 1985. The use of the names and addresses of cable subscribers for direct mail marketing purposes remains a critical issue there.

Federal Legislation: The Cable Communications Policy Act of 1984

Until 1983 there was little federal action on cable privacy, largely because of the deregulatory inclinations of the Reagan administration. In testimony before a Senate subcommittee on April 26, 1982, Mark S. Fowler, Chairman of the Federal Communications Commission (FCC), asserted that "it is essential to recognize that the principal arena of cable regulation is, and should continue to be, at the non-federal level." Fowler is also reported to have stated that the FCC regarded cable privacy as an issue not yet calling for federal action.[20]

In general, according to Gardner and White, representatives of American cable television companies "seem to be seeking to avoid any new statutory restrictions on their ability to collect, store and utilize personal data as they see fit." These authors argue that federal regulation will ultimately be essential for cable privacy in the United States, since "the decentralized regulation of communications and information networks runs counter to technological innovation and implementation."[21] Fred Weingarten of the U.S. Office of Technology Assessment has suggested that industry pressure for federal legislation will increase as cable companies begin to see themselves whipsawed by a variety of state and municipal regulations.[22]

Two bills that touched on cable privacy were introduced into the U.S. Senate in 1982. Senator Barry M. Goldwater introduced S. 2172, the Cable Telecommunications Act of 1982, and Senator Ernest F. Hollings introduced S. 2445, which has similar provisions on personal privacy. The National Cable

Television Association opposed these legislative measures, arguing the lack of any documentation of privacy abuse. On July 22, 1982 the Senate Commerce Committee voted 13 to three in favor of S. 2172, including those sections which provide protection for the privacy of cable subscribers. As *Privacy Times* noted, the privacy provisions are some of the least controversial aspects of the proposed measure, since they deal largely with the power of local authorities to regulate the cable industry.[23]

In late January 1983 Senator Howard Baker, acting for Senator Goldwater, reintroduced S. 2172 as S. 66. On April 21, 1983 the Senate Commerce Committee approved a compromise version of S. 66 by a vote of 15 to two. The Senate passed this Cable Telecommunications Act on June 14, 1983, thereby voicing its support of new cable technologies by removing the threat of conflicting city and municipal regulations. The deregulation bill for cable was vigorously opposed by the American Telephone and Telegraph Company.[24]

The New York Times described the Senate bill as "the first comprehensive legislation to establish a national framework for regulating the expanding cable industry." While it continues the power of cities to issue monopolies to cable operators, it also limits their power over cable networks. Section 610 of S. 2172 and S. 66 concerns the protection of subscriber privacy. It forbids the use of the cable system "to collect personally identifiable information with respect to a cable subscriber, except upon the prior written consent of that subscriber," unless the information is used solely for billing purposes or to monitor for unauthorized reception of cable services. In addition, any data collected have to be destroyed "when the information is no longer used or to be used for the purposes for which it was collected." Personal information collected by the cable system in identifiable form shall not be disclosed "except upon the prior written consent of the subscriber, or pursuant to a lawful court order authorizing such disclosure." The proposed bills further provide for notice to the cable subscriber concerned, if a court has authorized or ordered disclosure. Finally, a cable subscriber is entitled to recover civil damages for violation of his or her privacy.

The Videotex Industry Association lobbied for certain changes in S. 66, since it would apply to videotex services operating over cable. The bill was revised to allow subscribers to give informed consent electronically and to permit cable systems to collect identifiable microdata on subscribers for market research.

The protections for subscriber privacy in S. 2172 and S. 66 were not controversial. They "reflect the Committee's belief that the development of new and diversified services over interactive two-way cable systems should not impact adversely upon the privacy of the individual. This section is not intended to impose unreasonable requirements. The Committee believes that potentially, the principal problem is the opportunity to monitor subscriber viewing habits and disclose personally identifiable information without prior consent. Section 610 provides the necessary protection in this area.[25]

The House of Representatives considered a counterpart bill, H.R. 4103, to the proposed Senate legislation. Its provisions on privacy were very similar to S. 66. The House Telecommunications Subcommittee approved the bill on November 17, 1983. "The Cable Communications Policy Act of 1984" was reported out of the House Energy and Commerce Committee in late June 1984, passed Congress in October and was signed into law by President Reagan on October 30. There was some opposition by the cable television industry and the Direct Mail Marketing Association to the admirable provisions on the protection of subscriber privacy in Section 631 of the bill.[26]

Section 631 of the Cable Communications Policy Act of 1984 covers privacy matters more fully than the earlier House and Senate versions of the bill. Cable operators have to provide subscribers to cable television services with a separate annual written statement, which clearly and conspicuously states the nature, uses, disclosures, retention periods and rights of access concerning the identifiable personal information to be collected with respect to the subscriber. A subscriber has to furnish prior written or electronic consent before a cable operator can use the cable system for the collection and disclosure of identifiable personal information, except that the cable company may collect, use and disclose personal information in order to provide legitimate business services to the subscriber or to respond to a court order, and may disclose names and addresses, if the subscriber has had an opportunity to prohibit or limit such disclosure. Any person aggrieved by any act of a cable operator in violation of Section 631 may bring a civil action, and a United States district court may award actual damages, punitive damages, and reasonable attorneys' fees and other litigation costs. The federal measures on cable privacy do not prohibit any state or any franchising authority from enacting or enforcing laws consistent with Section 631 for the protection of subscriber privacy.

Finally, the provisions on subscriber privacy conclude with strong controls on government access to personally identifiable information on a cable subscriber. A "governmental entity" may obtain such access pursuant to a court order, only if in a court proceeding it has offered "clear and convincing evidence" that the subject of the information is reasonably suspected of engaging in criminal activity, that the information sought would be material evidence in the case, and that the subject of the information is afforded the opportunity to appear and contest such entity's claim.

REGULATION OF THE U.S. TELEPHONE INDUSTRY

The various types of problems for privacy and confidentiality that arise in private telephone service are largely left to be dealt with through self-regulation by the telephone industry, despite the existence of some controlling statutes and court decisions at the federal and state levels. American Telephone and Telegraph Company (AT&T) has taken many steps to develop a strong privacy program, but the entire issue deserves reconsideration now that the 23 regional operating telephone companies have been divested by AT&T and reorganized into seven independent corporate entities. It is vital that AT&T policies be fully continued by the new companies, especially considering that privacy advocates continue to be dissatisfied with the overall amount of "telephone privacy" available in the United States.[27]

Over the years, AT&T has continued to express its strong commitment to the protection of its customers' communications and business records, arguing that the preservation of privacy is a basic concept in the telephone business. In 1977 it created a Bell System Employee Privacy Protection Committee to formalize its record-keeping policies and practices; the Committee produced a comprehensive statement of employee privacy policy and detailed companion guidelines for implementation. The document, which runs some 70 pages, was implemented by all Bell Companies by January 1, 1980.[28] Each company has its own Privacy Coordinator, whose responsibility it is to oversee the effective implementation of the privacy program. AT&T also has issued an employee handbook, recently revised for the fourth time in eight years, that has an up-to-date statement on "privacy of communication." It covers, for example, the protection of transmission either by voice or by data or other non-voice communications.[29]

In 1977 the Privacy Protection Study Commission in the U.S. recommended that an individual should have an enforceable statutory expectation of confidentiality in records of long-distance telephone service.[30] This continues to be a significant issue of concern to privacy advocates, who are worried about unauthorized, illegal and informal ways of obtaining access to personal information of various types.[31]

AT&T and Bell System Companies in the U.S. have a 21-page document covering the release of toll billing record information to third parties.[32] Such records are normally destroyed as a matter of routine business practice at the end of a six-month period. They are only disclosed to third parties in response to subpoena, administrative summons, or court order valid on its face, and notice to customers in such instances is normal. There are the usual exceptions for law enforcement investigations and national security.

Although it is evident that AT&T and its former operating companies had made considerable strides in self-regulation, customers of telephone companies need reassurance about the existence and enforcement of such strong privacy programs and may also need further common law and statutory guarantees of their privacy rights in this area.

The argument for the need for stronger formal protections for the confidentiality of telephone records has useful precedents in recent California experience. In two 1981 decisions the California Public Utilities Commission, which regulates telephone companies, required them "to publish a set of uniform tariff rules governing the release of nonpublished information (unlisted telephone numbers and corresponding names and addresses) and the release of subscriber credit information and subscriber calling records." The Commission required the establishment of these uniform rules because the existing lack of uniformity and detail in telephone company tariff rules led to public misconception and dissatisfaction concerning the degree of privacy accorded this subscriber information.[33]

On April 26, 1984 the California Supreme Court further ruled in a unanimous decision that the California Constitution protects the privacy of telephone records: "The fact that a significant percentage of customers take affirmative steps to keep their names, addresses and telephone numbers confidential demonstrates the importance of this privacy interest to a large portion of the population. Under these circumstances, an expectation of privacy was reasonable." As *Privacy Times* pointed out on May 9, 1984, this decision is at odds with the U.S. Supreme Court's holdings that individuals do not have a legitimate expectation of privacy in their records when they are maintained by third parties, "and that privacy interests are surrendered when one opens a bank account or acquires a phone. Thus, Californians have a stronger privacy interest in their personal files than do other Americans."

Bills on telephone privacy have been proposed in Congress in recent years, but have made little progress because of lack of interest. In 1983, Congressman Ted Weiss of New York introduced H.R. 424, the Federal Privacy of Telephone Records Act. Its purposes were "(1) to protect the privacy of telecommunications records from unwarranted disclosure; and (2) to limit intrusion into personal privacy even where disclosure to government is deemed appropriate." H.R. 424 proposed amendments to the Communications Act of 1934 which would have applied to both telephone and cable companies as "service providers."

NOTES

1. The provisions on tapping in the Minneapolis Franchise Ordinance, Section 99C-9D, and in the Portland Franchise Ordinance, Section 13.2, are very similar to the Syracuse provision.

2. Warner Amex Cable Communications, Inc., *Code of Privacy* (New York, 1981).

3. Communication to author from Ronald L. Plesser, June 8, 1982.

4. These model videotex privacy guidelines are printed in full in Appendix A at the end of this volume.

5. Alan F. Westin, "Home Information Systems: The Privacy Debate," *Datamation*, XXVIII, No. 7 (July 1982), p. 104.

6. *News from Attorney General Robert Abrams,* May 6, 1982.

7. Sidney L. Gardner and Robin White, *New Technology and the Right to Privacy: State Responses to Federal Inaction. A Report to the New York State Consumer Protection Board.* (Unpublished draft, August 1982), p. 72.

8. Robert Ellis Smith, "One Perspective on Warner Amex Cable," *Privacy Journal,* IX (February 1983), p. 6.

9. Gardner and White, *New Technology and the Right to Privacy,* pp. 69–70.

10. Westin, "Home Information Systems: The Privacy Debate," *Datamation,* XXVIII. p. 112.

11. The Communications Consumer Privacy Act, 1981, *Ill. Legis. Serv.* P.A. 82-526 (West), and *Ill. Ann. Stat.,* c. 38, s. 87-1 *et seq.,* ss. 1, 3 and 3(b).

12. Wisconsin, Laws of 1981, c. 271, ss. 1, 2.

13. I am most grateful to Alan F. Westin for furnishing me with the information used in this paragraph.

14. California, Laws of 1982, Chapter 1519, 1982 *Cal. Legis. Serv.* 8220 (West); *Privacy Journal,* VIII (September 1982), pp. 1, 5; *Privacy Journal,* VIII (October 1982), p. 6.

15. The mere fact that an individual is a cable television subscriber is not "identifiable individual information" under the law. (California, Laws of 1982, c. 1519, s. 1.)

16. *Connecticut General Statutes Annotated* (St. Paul, MN, West Publishing Co., 1984), IX, p. 282.

17. Joseph I. Lieberman, "TV's Watching You," *The New York Times,* May 31, 1983, p. A20; and letter-to-the-editor by Henry F. Mazel, *The New York Times,* June 13, 1983, p. A14.

18. *The New York Times,* February 16, 1982, p. A18; WABC-TV, New York City, editorial, February 19–21, 1982; WNBC-TV, New York City, editorial, January 29, 1982.

19. State of New York Commission on Cable Television, "Notice of Proposed Rulemaking," Docket No. 90221, adopted February 23, 1983 and released March 3, 1983.

20. Gardner and White, *New Technology and the Right to Privacy*, p. 14; Westin, "Home Information Systems: The Privacy Debate," *Datamation* XXVIII, p. 111. See also Sally Bedell, "An F.C.C. Chief in an Era of Broadcasting Change," *The New York Times*, February 22, 1983, p. C20.

21. Gardner and White, *New Technology and the Right to Privacy*, pp. 14, 25. Several recent articles also argue for federal cable privacy legislation: Gary Selvin, "As Interactive Cable Enters, Does Privacy Go Out the Window?" *Journal of Communications and Entertainment Law*, IV (1982), 781–792; Frank W. Lloyd, "Cable Television's Emerging Two-Way Services: A Dilemma for Federal and State Regulators," *Vanderbilt Law Review*, XXXVI (1983), pp. 1045–91; and Stephen Console, "Cable Television Privacy Act: Protecting Privacy Interests from Cable TV Technology," *Federal Communications Law Journal*, XXXV (1983), pp. 71–94. The latter includes draft legislation and explanatory comment.

22. Communication to author from Fred Weingarten, May 21, 1982.

23. *Privacy Journal*, VIII, No. 8 (June 1982), p. 5; Gardner and White, *New Technology and the Right to Privacy*, p. 15 (these authors describe the two Senate bills on cable privacy as "weak"; see p. 17); *Privacy Times*, II, No. 15 (August 4, 1982), p. 1.

24. *Cable Telecommunications Act of 1982. Report together with Additional Views of the Senate Committee on Commerce, Science, and Transportation on S. 2172.* Rept. No. 97-518. 97th Congress, 2nd Sess. (Washington, DC, August 10, 1982), pp. 40–41; 98th Congress, 1st Sess., S. 66 to amend the Communications Act of 1934, s. 610; *The New York Times*, June 15, 1983, p. D1; Sally Bedell Smith, "Cable-TV Industry to Press Decontrol Measure in House," *The New York Times*, June 16, 1983, p. D4; and *Privacy Journal*, IX (May 1983), p. 5.

25. *Cable Telecommunications Act of 1982*, p. 21.

26. *Privacy Times*, III (November 16, 1983), pp. 1–2.

27. See Robert Ellis Smith, *Privacy. How to Protect What's Left of It* (Garden City, NY: Anchor Press/Doubleday, 1979), pp. 189–197.

28. This discussion is based on a presentation by AT&T attorney, H.W. William Caming, "The Protection of Transborder Data Information in the United States," to the Legal Symposium on International Information Networks, Geneva, Switzerland, October 28, 1983, as part of International Telecommunication Union's "Telecom '83."

29. See AT&T, *A Personal Responsibility* (April 1983), pp. 2, 7.

30. U.S. Privacy Protection Study Commission, *Personal Privacy in an Information Society* (Washington, DC: U.S. Government Printing Office, July 1977), pp. 21, also 27, 356.

31. See *Privacy Times,* II, No. 5 (August 4, 1982), pp. 2–3.

32. See AT&T, *Privacy Guidelines for Bell System Security Organizations,* Section I, "Bell System Policy and Procedures for the Release of Toll Billing Record Information," (July 1982).

33. See Decision No. 93361, dated July 22, 1981, and Decision No. 83-06-066, dated June 15, 1983, before the Public Utilities Commission of the State of California. Appendix B of Decision No. 93361 sets forth the rules under which telephone companies may release subscriber credit information and subscriber calling records.

6

International Initiatives in Data Protection

At the present time, European countries are in a better position to respond to personal privacy issues raised by new information technology than are the United States and Canada. Any emerging problem in France, Sweden or West Germany, for example, can be turned over to existing data protection agencies for review, evaluation and appropriate recommendations, since such agencies have either licensing or advisory functions which apply to new personal information systems.

WEST GERMANY

In West Germany—particularly in Dusseldorf—a variety of experiments with two-way videotex services are underway. Ongoing disputes between the federal government and the Länder about jurisdiction over cable were resolved in 1983. The heads of the 11 state governments signed a public law contract for videotex on March 18, 1983, which is now being ratified by the respective legislatures. The agreement includes specific provisions for data protection, limiting and controlling the collection and storage of identifiable personal data, and preventing the creation of profiles of those who use information-retrieval services.

The Third Activity Report for 1980 of the Federal Data Protection Commissioner reviewed his activities in connection with the Federal Postal Administration (PTT) and the new media. Some of the sensitive privacy issues in West Germany are increased by the fact that the postal, telegraph and telephone systems are owned by the government. In his 1980 report, then Commissioner Professor Hans-Peter Bull concluded that data protection considerations must be accounted for before a *fait accompli* exists.[1]

Professor Bull also drew attention to the "principles of data protection in the new media, in particular teletext and cable television," which were drawn up by a joint working group composed of state data protection commissioners and representatives of his federal office and approved at their Seventh Joint Conference on December 11, 1980.[2] The commissioners determined that data protection issues should be resolved at the time that the two-way experiments were initiated rather than after they were already in operation. According to the principles they ratified, personal data on subscribers can be collected and stored only if essential and necessary for the performance of the service in question. Generally, subscriber consent is necessary for the storage of personal information. But under West German constitutional provisions for the protection of privacy, storage of certain sensitive data would not be permitted, even if the subscriber consented. For the so-called "feedback channel," data may be stored only for the purpose for which they were initially disclosed. The principles forbid the storage "of data on subscribers in a form which allows the formation of a personality profile. . . ."

INTERNATIONAL GUIDELINES

The International Conference of Data Protection Commissioners unanimously adopted resolutions on the new electronic media at their annual meeting in Stockholm in October 1983. The commissioners from Western Europe and Canada agreed "that the application of new media disseminated by cable networks may involve a considerable hazard to the personal right of privacy."[3] They were particularly concerned that the automatic collection of personal data would make possible the creation of personality profiles of all users. The conference concluded that each country should take appropriate action, especially by means of legislation, to ensure that the operation of the new media does not infringe on personal privacy. The commissioners recommended restricting the collection, storage and communication of personal data to the lowest possible level of utilization and prohibiting the compilation of personality profiles. In terms of the risk of transferring personal information across national borders, the commissioners recommended adherence to the minimum standards for the protection of individuals set forth by the Council of Europe's 1981 Convention[4] and the guidelines developed by the Organization for Economic Co-operation and Development (OECD) in 1980. Finally, the commissioners concluded that their data protection agencies should cooperate internationally in the supervision of the new media.

The OECD guidelines for member countries are designed to apply to personal data, "whether in the public or private sectors, which, because of the manner in which they are processed, or because of their nature or the context in which they are used, pose a danger to privacy and individual liberties."[5]

The principles of fair information practices most relevant to two-way services in the OECD guidelines are the following:

7. There should be limits to the collection of personal data and any such data should be obtained by lawful and fair means and, where appropriate, with the knowledge or consent of the data subject.

9. The purposes for which data are collected should be specified not later than at the time of data collection and the subsequent use limited to the fulfillment of those purposes or such others as are not incompatible with those purposes and as are specified on each occasion of change of purpose.

10. Personal data should not be disclosed, made available or otherwise used for purposes other than those specified in accordance with Paragraph 9 except: a) with the consent of the data subject; or b) by the authority of law.

Further principles in the OECD guidelines concern security safeguards, openness about developments, access by the individual to data and accountability.[6] The guidelines on implementation of data protection in Section 19 urge member countries to "encourage and support self-regulation, whether in the form of codes of conduct or otherwise. . .[and to] provide for adequate sanctions and remedies in case of failures to comply with measures which implement the principles set forth in Parts Two and Three. . ."

The U.S. is a signatory to the OECD guidelines. The Canadian federal government only formally adhered to the basic data protection principles contained in the guidelines on June 29, 1984. It will now undertake a program to encourage private sector corporations to develop and implement voluntary privacy protection codes. Earlier, at least 100 major multinational corporations in the U.S. advised the Secretary of Commerce in 1981 of their voluntary compliance with these guidelines for their data processing and data collection activities. Thus, the OECD guidelines should serve as an additional model for voluntary data protection activities on the part of U.S. and Canadian companies offering two-way services.

ACTIVITIES IN GREAT BRITAIN

On October 12, 1982 the Home Office in Great Britain released the report of the inquiry chaired by Lord Hunt of Tanworth on the wiring of the country for cable. The thrust of the recommendations to the British government was to encourage the laying of cable as quickly and with as little regulation as possible. The Hunt inquiry, it should be noted, was well aware of the prospects for introducing "channels with two-way communications capability ('interactive') allowing information to pass in both directions," including such services as opinion-polling, security services, information exchanges, telebanking and electronic mail. It was also aware that two-way cable services could lead to "risks to privacy. . . ." Nevertheless, the report concluded that "the award of franchises should positively encourage the development of the interactive services."[7]

On April 27, 1983 the Conservative government of Prime Minister Thatcher published a White Paper on cable television described by *The Economist* as "a Magna Charta for cable." Once again, the recommendations encouraged cabling by the private sector with as few restrictions as possible. A statutory cable authority under a pending Cable and Broadcasting bill will be instructed to rule with a light hand. The White Paper also proposes to allow the introduction of pay-per-view services. The technology to be used for the cable system must be interactive on some channels. The government granted interim licenses to 11 consortia of applicants at the end of November 1983. The winning bidders included American, but not Canadian, multi-system operators.[8]

The White Paper on cable television indicated an awareness of the risks to privacy, especially with the sensitive data available from telebanking and teleshopping. The government indicated that it would rely on its pending Data Protection Bill to "provide significant safeguards against the misuse of cable systems for infringing individual privacy," and would consider the need for additional protections if the need arose.[9]

A commitment by the Thatcher government to go forward with data protection legislation similar to that in effect in other European countries accompanied the decision on wiring Great Britain. The House of Lords passed a Data Protection Bill in March 1983; it was reintroduced on June 23 after the general election and passed again on November 3, 1983. The bill has been approved by the House of Commons and is expected to come into force in 1985. It is a complex piece of legislation that establishes, among other things, an independent Data Protection Registrar with a staff of 20 non-civil servants, who will register all users of automated personal information systems in the public and private sectors.[10] Such a licensing requirement has not previously been used in data protection legislation for an English-speaking country, especially not for the private sector.

Schedule 1 of the Data Protection Law sets forth the traditional data protection principles contained in all national data protection laws and in the OECD guidelines. The task of the registrar is to ensure that all data users, such as cable companies, comply with the principles in their handling of personal data. Clause 5 makes it a criminal offense to hold personal data without being registered or knowingly or recklessly to hold, use, obtain, disclose or transfer such data otherwise than as specified in the registered entry. The registrar may even refuse to register a data user, if he or she is satisfied "that the applicant is likely to contravene any of the data protection principles." Alternatively, a company may be de-registered for noncompliance with the principles. Data subjects have the right to be informed that data about them are being collected, and the right to sue for damages if their data are disclosed without authority.[11] A company or an individual may appeal a decision of the registrar to a Data Protection Tribunal and to the courts. Thus, companies offering interactive services in the United Kingdom will have to conform to data protection standards set by a government regulatory regime.

Technological and regulatory advances in the U.K. testify to both current and future developments in other English-speaking countries. In fact, the British decision to adopt the model of a European-style data protection commissioner, even if undertaken for purely economic reasons of permitting transborder data flows, has significant implications for the U.S. and Canada. Up to now, the U.S. federal government and every state except New York has regarded the creation of a data protection commission or commissioner as unnecessary, even for the public sector. Canadian provinces (excluding Quebec) have to date been able to argue that a data protection commission or commissioner was not in the English common law or legislative tradition, particularly in terms of giving a commissioner independence from ministerial control. It should now be more difficult for both countries to resist the creation of regulatory systems for data protection in both the public and private sectors, which include an oversight body such as a Privacy Protection Commission.

This brief detour into data protection developments in Western Europe suggests the extent to which appropriate provisions for data protection in the private sector are sorely lacking in North America at either the federal, state or provincial levels. Although privacy can perhaps best be ensured by data protection tailored to specific interactive services, neither the companies nor regulatory authorities can continue to claim that they lack appropriate models. The prospect of universal data protection schemes affecting the private sector, such as those being carried out in the United Kingdom, should be a strong incentive for companies offering interactive services to self-regulate at the least.

NOTES

1. *Dritter Tätigkeitsbericht des Bundesbeauftragten für den Datenschutz* (*Third Activity Report of the Federal Data Protection Commissioner*), (Bonn, 1980), s. 3.7. I am most grateful to Herr Herbert Burkert of the Gesellschaft für Mathematik und Datenverarbeitung (GMD) in Bonn for continued guidance on the West German situation.

2. *Ibid.*, s. 3.8.2 and Appendix 2. These principles have been translated into English by the Berlin Data Protection Commissioner in a version dated January 21, 1981.

3. The text of the resolutions can be found in *Transnational Data Report*, VI, No. 8 (December 1983), p. 416.

4. Council of Europe, *Explanatory Report on the Convention for the Protection of Individuals with Regard to Automatic Processing of Personal Data* (Strasbourg: Council of Europe, 1981).

5. Organization for Economic Co-operation and Development, *Guidelines for the Protection of Privacy and Transborder Flows of Personal Data* (Paris: OECD, 1981), s. 2.

6. *Ibid.*, s. 11–14.

7. Home Office, *Report of the Inquiry into Cable Expansion and Broadcasting Policy* (Cmnd. 8679, London, U.K.: Her Majesty's Stationery Office, October 1982), p. 2.

8. Home Office, *The Development of Cable Systems and Services* (Cmnd. 8866, London, U.K.: Her Majesty's Stationery Office, April 1983), pp. 8, 47–49; *The Economist,* April 30, 1983, pp. 9–10, 71–72; *The Financial Post,* December 10, 1983, p. 18.

9. Home Office, *The Development of Cable Systems and Services,* pp. 67, 86, 166.

10. Background information on the legislation can be found in the slender White Paper published on April 7, 1982: *Data Protection: The Government Proposals for Legislation* (Cmnd. 8539, London, U.K.: Her Majesty's Stationery Office, April 7, 1982).

11. Data Protection Bill [H.L.], clauses 5(1), 5(5), 7(2)(b), 11(1), 21(1)(a), and 23(1)(c). See Bryan Niblett, *Data Protection Act 1984* (London: Oyez Longman, 1984).

7

Canadian Regulatory Options

THE CANADIAN RADIO-TELEVISION AND
TELECOMMUNICATIONS COMMISSION (CRTC)

The Canadian cable television industry is the major agent for the implementation and achievement of the new "broadcasting strategy for Canada" announced by the Minister of Communications on March 1, 1983. The new policy encourages the introduction of various types of non-programming cable services, including videotex, security services and information retrieval, and ensures that the CRTC has clear authority to regulate all cable operations. In February 1984 the government also introduced Bill C-20, empowering the Cabinet to issue legally binding policy directives to the CRTC, but the bill failed to pass before Parliament was dissolved in July 1984 for an election.[1]

The CRTC currently licenses and regulates the Canadian cable television industry. Each local cable company has a designated territory authorized by the CRTC. Detailed regulations govern its operating practices and subscription rates. At regular intervals a local company must apply for renewal of its license. Thus, at present, almost every aspect of the conduct of a cable television operation in Canada comes under the jurisdiction of the CRTC.[2]

Since it came into existence on April 1, 1968, the CRTC has become one of the most visible of the federal regulatory tribunals. Its jurisdiction over cable television activities stems from the Broadcasting Act of 1968.[3] But, as will be discussed further below, the Broadcasting Act, which has not been revised since its creation, does not explicitly establish the jurisdiction of the CRTC over the type of two-way services currently being contemplated by cable companies. Section three of the Act sets forth the objectives for Canadian broadcasting policy, none of which, it can be argued, relate directly to non-programming services. Yet the CRTC has a statutory mandate to "regulate and supervise all aspects of the Canadian broadcasting system with a view to implementing the broadcasting policy enunciated in Section Three of this Act." It also has statutory power to "make regulations applicable to all

115

persons holding broadcasting licenses" concerning a specified range of subjects and "respecting such other matters as it deems necessary for the furtherance of its objects."[4]

Under the Broadcasting Act, the CRTC issues Cable Television Regulations which deal primarily with television service priorities, the allocation of television channels, the use of the community channel and radio service priorities. The regulations do specify that "a licensee shall not use, or permit the use of, its undertaking or any channel of its undertaking except as required or authorized by its license for these Regulations."[5]

Strong basic disagreements exist between the federal government and the Canadian provinces as to who should have broad jurisdiction over cable television. At the annual meeting of the Ontario Cable Television Association on October 20, 1982, the Communications Ministers for British Columbia and Saskatchewan indicated their belief that their provinces had jurisdiction over cable enterprises. The Ontario Transportation and Communications Minister, James Snow, stated that his province had been expecting for some time to obtain jurisdiction over the cable industry on the basis of negotiations with the liberal government, but the prospects seemed minimal.[6] Many provincial governments believe that the delivery of non-programming services over cable systems does not constitute "broadcasting" under the division of powers of the Canadian constitution. The problem for the cable companies is that they may thus find themselves having to respond to two levels of regulation. As is also true in the U.S., the major Canadian cable system operators see direct benefits in having one level of regulation by the federal government.

Jurisdiction of the CRTC

If these disputes over jurisdiction are essentially political in character, they in fact have a legal and constitutional basis. The legal jurisdiction of the CRTC over interactive cable television services is somewhat questionable, and it is arguable that a licensee could win a court test of the CRTC's jurisdiction to license and regulate non-programming services. But no company has challenged the several sets of CRTC licensing decisions to date, including a decision to prohibit cable companies from carrying classified real estate advertising.[7]

Since the CRTC faces a tremendous volume of work because of its licensing functions in broadcasting, cable television and telecommunications, its large staff of more than 400 plays a fundamental role in the development of CRTC policies, although decisions are made at a higher level. It is sufficient to note here that there is a considerable difference of opinion within the CRTC as to whether section three of the Broadcasting Act grants the agency jurisdiction over non-programming services or over matters concerning the protection of personal privacy in such services. Because privacy protection is not a power specifically enumerated in the Act, should the CRTC prescribe detailed procedures for cable companies to undertake with respect to the protection of personal privacy, the cable industry could in theory challenge such jurisdiction in the courts. Some CRTC staff members feel that section three of the Broadcasting Act does not pose any insurmountable problems with respect to regulating two-way cable services and privacy. Moreover, since the Act has been under revision for almost a decade, it is also plausible that a revised act would be more explicit on this point.

Doubts as to whether the jurisdiction of the CRTC extends over every aspect of the cable television industry also tend to be reduced by the results of recent court decisions. Its jurisdiction was most recently upheld by the 1982 decision of the Court of Appeal of the Supreme Court of Newfoundland in the *Queen* v. *Shellbird Cable Limited,* and by the Supreme Court of Canada's refusal to hear an appeal in the case.[8] Shellbird, a Newfoundland cable television company located in Corner Brook, was charged with making unauthorized rebroadcasts of programs transmitted from Washington, DC, contrary to provisions of its CRTC license. Shellbird was in fact receiving the Public Broadcasting Service transmitted via an American satellite to an earth station in Corner Brook. A Provincial Court judge initially acquitted Shellbird of criminal charges. He determined that such an activity did not constitute "broadcasting" under the Broadcasting Act, and hence the CRTC lacked jurisdiction to prosecute Shellbird. The Attorney General of Canada subsequently appealed.

The Court of Appeal of Newfoundland concluded that the "objects of the Act set out in S.3. . .clearly refer not only to broadcast services but also to non-broadcast services, provided they are carried as a broadcasting undertaking, [and] that this position is reinforced by the language of S.15 of the Broadcasting Act." Speaking for the court, Chief Justice Mifflin concluded that in his view "the total programming carried by a licensed broadcasting undertaking must be governed by its license to operate whether or not a given program comes within the definition of broadcasting. To exempt programs which do not fall within the strict definition of broadcasting from regulation by the Commission, would be contrary to the policy of this Act as set out in S.3 and it would ultimately defeat the whole purpose of having a national broadcasting policy for which the statute was enacted."

More recently, Northern Cablevision Limited of Grande Prairie, Alberta, pleaded guilty in Alberta Provincial Court to six counts of distributing a broadcasting service for which it was not licensed by the CRTC. The prosecution had apparently been delayed until the release of the *Shellbird* decision. A spokesman for the federal Department of Communications claimed that the Northern Cablevision case was very similar to the Shellbird case and that it reconfirmed the jurisdiction of the CRTC.[9]

At the annual meeting of the Canadian Cable Television Association (CCTA) in Vancouver in May 1980, Charles Dalfen, then vice-chairman of the CRTC, reminded cable television companies that they remained broadcasting undertakings under the law. Thus, under the current Broadcasting Act, cable companies have no choice but to obtain a CRTC license to offer any cable service. It is also relevant that during hearings in Toronto and Vancouver in the spring of 1981 on non-programming services, senior representatives of the cable companies explictly acknowledged the jurisdiction of the CRTC over such services. In a discussion of whether or not non-programming services fell under the definition of a broadcast in the cable television regulations, John W. Graham, chairman of Rogers Cablesystems Inc., stated that Rogers will call such services whatever the CRTC wants them to be called: "I think the Commission generally refers to these as non-broadcasting services and with that category we are very happy to live because it provides you with jurisdiction and us with a track on which to run." When CRTC lawyer Bill Howard asked the cable companies whether they or a service provider would be responsible for the content of services furnished to a subscriber, Graham answered:

It is my understanding that the licensee of the broadcast receiving undertaking is responsible for everything that goes on his system. Having said that, there is no question that broadcast news, in fact, is responsible for the content of what goes on the news wire. Providers of other programs, in fact, are responsible for choosing what goes into their programs. Now, I don't say that...with any thought of lessening the ultimate bottom line liability of the licensee.[10]

At the Vancouver hearings Commissioner James Robson asked George Fierheller of Rogers what control the cable company would have over the teleshopping channel. Fierheller answered that the ultimate responsiblity would be with the CRTC. He noted that the local cable company, since it is a broadcasting undertaking, would have to live with whatever guidelines the CRTC provided.[11]

Cable Companies as Carriers

On what basis should the CRTC regulate Canadian cable television companies? Is a cable company best described as a "broadcasting undertaking" under the Broadcasting Act, or as a carrier, especially when it comes to the furnishing and delivery of two-way services? It is clear that developments in technology have overtaken the static language of the Broadcasting Act. It is equally clear that, traditional regulatory definitions notwithstanding, in offering a two-way service such as teleshopping or banking, a cable company is in reality serving primarily as a carrier between the service provider and the subscriber. Thus, certain aspects of two-way services clearly have "common carrier" characteristics. On the other hand, for such two-way services as pay-per-view television or public opinion-polling, the cable company is functioning not as a carrier but as the broadcaster, operator or information provider.

The problem becomes directly relevant to our line of discussion because at least one executive of a major Canadian multi-system operator would like to escape privacy regulation on the grounds that it is simply a common carrier like the telephone company. As such, a cable company might not be responsible for protecting the confidentiality of the personal information carried over its system.

During the 1981 CRTC hearings in Toronto and Vancouver, representatives of Rogers made it very clear that they did *not* regard themselves as common carriers: ". . .we have never claimed to be a carrier and we are not. We are broadcasters, always have been. . . ." This is the predominant view in the industry.

Intervenors from the private sector have also wanted assurances that a cable company would not be allowed to be in a position where it could prohibit access to cable facilities by other information and service providers.[12] As Charles Dalfen pointed out in May 1980, concern exists "about cable operators controlling both message and medium." In early 1981, after he had left the CRTC for private law practice, Dalfen noted in a research study for the Royal Commission on Newspapers that "in almost all respects, cable-TV is a 'hybrid' phenomenon, combining activities associated with both broadcasting and common carriage, and with the attendant public interest responsibilities of both." It is a matter of continuing active debate as to which characterization is the more appropriate. Dalfen noted that "with the development of a growing number of non-broadcasting related services, the justification for regulating cable—particularly as part of the broadcasting system—will no doubt have to be reconsidered."[13]

The CRTC has stated that "although not a broadcaster, cable television is not a common carrier either. . . . Indeed, as a licensed broadcasting receiving undertaking it is legally responsible for the contents of its messages. . . .In essence, while exhibiting characteristics both of the broadcaster and the common carrier, cable television remains hybrid in nature."[14] There is thus general acceptance at present that the CRTC will hold cable companies responsible for the information contents of their systems. It should be noted that the Hunt Inquiry in Britain also concluded that the cable operator, not the service provider, should be held "responsible for the programmes and services he distributes."[15]

CRTC Initiatives in Regulating Non-Programming Services

The question of the jurisdiction of the CRTC over cable privacy is indeed complicated and somewhat controversial. Nevertheless, it is meaningful for our purposes to evaluate the prospects for CRTC initiatives in this area. Despite the problems already discussed, the simplest way to deal with cable privacy in Canada would be for the CRTC to require appropriate protective requirements in the licenses it issues to each local cable company. But, for a number of reasons, including jurisdictional disputes and its current regulatory burden, the CRTC is somewhat reluctant to act.

Despite questions about its jurisdiction and about the principles involved in regulation, the CRTC has taken the initiative since 1978 to regulate what it calls "non-programming services." It has licensed a variety of such services for a two-year experimental period to the end of 1983, which has now been extended into 1985. The process began with the public announcement on June 6, 1978 entitled "Non-programming Services by Cable Television Licensees." The CRTC essentially stated that it would "give prompt and favorable consideration to applications by cable television licensees for the use of their systems to provide new communications services of a non-programming nature." The statement began with a citation from Section 5 of the *Cable Television Regulations,* which provides that a licensee shall not use its undertaking except as authorized by its license or the Regulations. The CRTC thus asserted jurisdiction over non-programming services for reasons that had nothing to do with the protection of personal privacy, but rather with the maintenance of the integrity of the broadcasting system. The Commission asserted that it had no intention "to inhibit the initiative of and the development of innovative services by the Canadian cable television industry."[16] Indeed, it noted that Section 3(j) of the Broadcasting Act calls for regulation that is "flexible and readily adaptable to scientific and technical advances."

The announcement led to a public hearing on November 21, 1978 in connection with applications for the distribution of such new services as burglar, fire and medical alarms, and information retrieval services. The telecommunications carriers in particular attacked the jurisdiction of the CRTC to approve the new services being requested by cable licensees. In a subsequent public statement on March 26, 1979 the CRTC responded that "the fact that broadcasting receiving undertakings may distribute non-programming services does not, in the Commission's view, alter its jurisdiction over the undertakings, so long as their reliance on television signals and on their ability to receive and transmit such signals to their subscribers is clear." The CRTC also noted, perhaps surprisingly, that:

> As the June 6 announcement indicated, the Commission does not intend to regulate non-programming services as such. Rather, it

views the applications for such services as requests to utilize the channel capacity of the cable television undertakings in question that is not at present required for off-air and locally originated programming services. The Commission considers that such utilization of the undertakings is consistent with Section 3(j) of the Broadcasting Act. However, the Commission requires that a cable television licensee wishing to introduce a non-programming service obtain authorization, in order that the Commission can satisfy itself that the introduction of the new service will not adversely affect the achievements of all the other objectives of the Broadcasting Act.[17]

The basic principles motivating the CRTC were the priority of programming services and the avoidance of a cross-subsidy to non-programming services from programming services by cable companies.

The March 1979 public statement accompanied a CRTC decision licensing non-programming services in a number of Canadian communities until March 31, 1982.[18] Ottawa Cablevision Limited was permitted to furnish burglar, fire and medical alarm systems. London (now Rogers) Cable TV was licensed to provide "communication services of a non-programming nature (fire and burglar/intrusion alarm, medical alert and security services) with subscriber involvement on a voluntary basis." (London Cable TV in fact introduced a channel-monitoring system and a public opinion-polling service.) None of the conditions for the experimental licenses had anything to do with data protection.

The CRTC subsequently held a series of four hearings on non-programming services in the spring of 1981 in Toronto, Vancouver, Calgary and Hull. The basic industry position could be described as a desire for licensing accompanied by only minimal regulation in accordance with the CRTC declaration that it did not intend to regulate non-programming services.[19] The CRTC announced its decisions to grant these varying licenses on December 31, 1981. Because the initial services authorized in 1979 had not advanced very far, the Commission granted a further trial period of an additional two years which would terminate on December 31, 1983. The CRTC concluded that it would eventually hold a public hearing "to assess the technological, economic, cultural and social impact of the services."[20]

The December 1981 decisions allowed the introduction of non-programming services by Telecable Videotron throughout the province of Quebec, and by Rogers-owned companies in Ontario, British Columbia and Alberta; also permitted was the introduction of surveillance security services on cable in communities in Alberta, Ontario and Manitoba.[21]

In its December 1981 public announcement the CRTC demonstrated relative insensitivity to the privacy issue by noting that, among all the non-programming services licensed, only opinion-polling raised specific problems. It simply stated that, in response to concerns expressed at the public hearings "about the dangers of putting such a vast amount of personal information in the hands of cable companies. . . the applicants confirmed that they would take all necessary precautions to ensure adequate safeguards to protect subscribers' privacy and security."

> In the Commission's view these monitoring services could give rise to serious social concerns if such safeguards are not carefully applied. In light of the implications relating to the security of information and to invasion of privacy, the Commission will only allow the cable distribution of such services if it is satisfied that proper mechanisms and safeguards are put in place. . . . Approval of the opinion-polling service is conditional upon licensees obtaining the prior agreement of each subscriber to be polled and, where appropriate, upon periodic or specific alerts being incorporated into this service to advise such subscribers that monitoring is being performed.[22]

Unfortunately, the official requirement in the December 1981 decisions that licensees implement proper safeguards to protect the privacy and security of subscribers did not extend to services other than opinion-polling.

The only subsequent move by the CRTC affecting non-programming services involved its decision of May 31, 1982 to extend the license of Telecable Videotron to September 30, 1986, well beyond the December 31, 1983 cut-off date for the other experimental licenses.[23] The rationale was that the proposed manufacturer of new interface equipment required a firm order for 100,000 units from Videotron, thus requiring a substantial and extended financial commitment by Videotron and the suppliers of non-programming services. Some observers wondered whether a system of non-programming services was any longer "experimental" when it was licensed for such a lengthy period.

CRTC Directives Regarding Data Protection

What should the CRTC be doing about the protection of privacy in interactive cable services? One starts with the assumption that the substantial burden of licensing, hearings and accompanying paperwork currently undertaken by the CRTC does not incline the organization to seek increased regulatory jurisdiction. Changing even the smallest of details in a license for a broadcasting receiving undertaking requires a further application, or at least notice, to the CRTC. Thus, the agency has had an understandable tendency to regard the protection of personal privacy as a policy issue whose time has not yet come. (As a policy issue, it would also necessitate the involvement of all 19 members of the Commission in any decision-making process, not just the Executive Committee.)

One goal of the several Canadian recommendations in this volume is to reduce to a minimum the additional regulatory burden placed on the CRTC. With this qualification in mind, the CRTC must nevertheless be persuaded that the protection of personal privacy, in both two-way cable television and telephone services, is a matter of sufficient importance to attract its continuing attention.

Especially in its December 1981 licensing decisions, the CRTC took certain basic steps towards the protection of personal privacy in two-way cable television services. More recently, on April 22, 1983, the CRTC determined that cable television licensees have to own and control the computer facility and security systems used to provide pay television services to cable TV subscribers.[24] But such measures are just a beginning. It is vital that the CRTC continue to develop a strong position on the privacy issue, partly because this is the easiest formal regulatory option available, given the current condition of cable television in Canada.

With respect to non-programming services, the CRTC has already built a case for the exercise of jurisdiction, as previously discussed. Thus, there seems to be no reason for the CRTC to adopt a minimalist position on data protection. If it develops a continuing will to act, few serious legal impediments exist to challenge its jurisdiction and those that do exist can be clarified by changes in the relevant federal statutes, if necessary. Since the federal Privacy Act of 1982 only regulates federal government data banks, it is also appropriate for the CRTC to deal with emerging privacy problems in the industries it regulates.

The CRTC hearings on two-way cable services originally planned for late 1983 were postponed, since not much progress had been made on the implementation of interactive services in Canada by that time. Since 1984 is focusing a great deal of attention on privacy questions, because of Orwell's famous novel, to hold such hearings during that year would have been most appropriate, but they are now tentatively scheduled for the spring of 1985. The hearings on non-programming services could serve as a prelude to the issuance of new licensing standards for two-way services designed to ensure the protection of privacy, confidentiality and physical security which could also incorporate the standards set by the cable television industry's efforts at self-regulation. Since each CRTC broadcasting license already includes a great deal of detail, a few additional clauses of this type will not be an imposing new burden.

Altering the existing experimental licenses for interactive services at the end of the licensing period also continues the established general CRTC practice of letting regulations evolve in response to experience. Because the cable companies were only granted licenses to operate on an experimental basis originally, the CRTC would have no difficulty in changing the rules in the licenses for non-programming services.

In a notice issued on October 26, 1983 the CRTC took its most decisive step to ensure appropriate data protection in two-way cable television services with the following declaration: "The Commission favors the development by the cable television industry of a voluntary code of minimum standards with a view to preventing all possible abuses relating to a subscriber's privacy." This conclusion followed a brief review of the ability of two-way cable services to gather personal information about individual subscribers. Possible abuses could occur if such information was transferred to third parties, "by sale or otherwise, even if in an aggregate form, without the consent or even the knowledge of the subscriber(s)." The CRTC "considers that subscribers' expectations [that] the confidentiality of all such information will be maintained places upon licensees the requirement of an unequivocal commitment to ensure subscriber privacy." Pending a more thorough review of the privacy issue in connection with cable carriage of non-programming services, the Commission reminded licensees "of their obligation to guarantee the privacy of their subscribers by measures which should include: informing subscribers of a system's relevant capabilities, obtaining prior subscriber consent for the collection of data, except that which is required for day-to-day operations, providing subscribers with reasonable access to personal records, assuring the security of such records, destroying those which are no longer needed and keeping individual subscriber data confidential."[25]

The CRTC thus directly encouraged the CCTA to pursue its initiative of forming an industry-wide committee to draft an appropriate privacy code, such as the one developed by the New York State Cable Television Association and the one under development by the U.S. National Cable Television Association. This approach might avoid the jurisdictional issues, since the cable television industry could voluntarily work with the CRTC on these questions, and, secondly, it combines self-regulation by the industry with a minimum role for the CRTC. (Based on precedents in other Canadian industry private-sector attempts at self-regulation, this activity alone would probably not be adequate to ensure data protection.)

A voluntary cable industry code on privacy still leaves open questions of enforcement, including the imposition of civil and criminal penalties such as those included in U.S. cable privacy acts. If, as a practical matter, the CRTC never takes away licenses, how could it fine a cable company? Such matters of enforcement will require further study.

CANADIAN FEDERAL LEGISLATION AND REGULATION

If the CRTC were unwilling to exercise jurisdiction over data protection problems in interactive services, other federal regulatory initiatives are still possible, including the development of data protection legislation for the private sector, the revision of the Broadcasting Act to cover privacy, or the inclusion of similar provisions in a new Telecommunications Act. Although federal as opposed to provincial regulation would be attractive for Canadian MSOs, the prospects for extensive federal intervention might encourage cable companies to adopt the necessary measures to self-regulate.

The Department of Communications has demonstrated little reluctance to intervene in any regulatory area. In fact, in introducing Bill C-43 (which includes the new Privacy Act) for third reading* in the House of Commons on June 28, 1982, Francis Fox, the Minister of Communications at that time, stated that "the next stage in the development of privacy legislation, [is] extension of the principles respecting the protection of personal information to the federally regulated private sector," which could include cable television and federally regulated telephone companies.[26]

The principles that the Minister referred to can be found in the federal Privacy Act passed by Parliament in July 1982.[27] In addition to incorporating the standard elements of a code of fair information practices, such as controls on the collection, use and disclosure of personal information, the Privacy Act considerably strengthens the responsibilities of the Privacy Commissioner to oversee information-handling activities relating to the protection of personal privacy at the federal level, including the initiation of investigations of particular issues. Since the new act was not passed in response to public pressure, but in recognition of the desirability of improved legislation by the Department of Justice and Members of Parliament, it is conceivable that similar statutory initiatives could be taken for the protection of privacy in the private sector. The jurisdiction of the Privacy Commissioner could be extended to the information-handling activities of the federally regulated private sector in the foreseeable future, especially now that the British government has taken its bold initiative in private-sector regulation (see Chapter 6).

Another federal solution to the problem of protecting individual privacy originated with a 1981 proposal by then Privacy Commissioner, Inger Hansen, Q.C., in her conclusion to an investigation of the problem of the social insurance number and its multiple uses. She advocated the amendment of the federal *Criminal Code* to create an offense "against the privacy of another."[28] Such an enactment would "require recipients or collectors of personal data. . . to disclose to the person providing the data all proposed uses of the data not already explicitly provided for or made compulsory by law. The disclosure should be at the time of collection, and consent to new uses would be necessary." An "offense against the privacy of another" would "prohibit the willful undisclosed acquisition, alteration, use, processing, manipulation, trans-

---

*The British parliamentary system requires three readings of any bill. The third reading represents the final step before passage of the legislation.

mission or destruction of personal data, not otherwise authorized by law, where the personal data are:"

> a) provided to obtain a benefit or service; b) provided under compulsion of law; or c) placed in the custody of another for storage and the exclusive use of the depositor, and where it is expressly or implicitly understood that the data will be kept confidential.

Hansen's proposal has the virtue of simplicity and deserves more attention and debate than it has received to date. Because the seriousness of the offense could vary, she recommended that an amendment to the *Criminal Code* provide for prosecution by way of summary proceedings or by indictment. Enforcement would be by means of the existing mechanisms for the enforcement of the criminal law, thus avoiding the necessity of creating a new bureaucracy. Perhaps the greatest advantage of making an action "against the privacy of another" a criminal offense is that its prohibitions would extend at once to both the public and private sectors.[29] Even the idea of creating such a criminal offense should stimulate the private sector into self-regulation designed to protect the privacy of personal information about individuals in all kinds of interactive systems. Cable company executives and staff might become surprisingly concerned about subscriber privacy were they to confront the prospect of criminal prosecution for misuse of personal data. It is worth noting that the new British Data Protection law includes criminal sanctions for abuses of personal information.

Pending Federal Legislation

A revision of the Broadcasting Act of 1968 has been underway for a number of years and may perhaps come to fruition, now that a new broadcasting strategy has been announced. The last version of a new Broadcasting Act, known as Bill C-16, the Telecommunications Bill, was introduced in the House of Commons on November 9, 1978. Its goal was to consolidate and clarify existing legislation into a single embodiment of national telecommunications law. New versions of Bill C-16 continue to be developed as a consolidation of existing law in a number of different areas, but have not yet been introduced in the House of Commons. Although Bill C-16 did not include any specific conditions concerning the protection of personal information in two-way services, there seems to be no reason why an appropriate clause on such a matter could not be included. If it seems impossible to work out an adequate system for sanctions and enforcement by means of cooperation between the cable television industry and the CRTC, then such provisions could be introduced in the revised Telecommunications Bill. One anticipates that the civil servants shaping the legislation in the Department of Communications and at least certain members of the House of Commons will be sympathetic to this approach, especially if self-regulation cannot settle all of the problems. There is also some evidence that the cable television industry would have less objection to the setting of statutory standards for the protection of the privacy of individuals using interactive services, if this was not accompanied by a federal bureaucracy to oversee implementation. This legislative approach may prove to be the most effective way to obtain adequate remedies in the courts for a subscriber whose privacy interests have been harmed.

In October 1983 the Department of Communications announced that it was undertaking a major review of telecommunications in order to revise federal legislation. The review will probably last several years and will include consultation with telephone and cable companies and the provinces. It will examine the role of the cable television industry as a common carrier and the prospect of permitting cable companies to provide a variety of two-way non-programming services. Although such a review will necessarily involve a myriad of issues, the Department of Communications should be encouraged to address issues of privacy and confidentiality of subscribers.[30]

PROVINCIAL LEGISLATION AND REGULATION

One can argue that privacy problems posed by interactive services should be dealt with by general solutions, such as the enactment of data protection laws at the provincial level, or by specific legislation dealing with cable privacy, as has been undertaken in the United States. Although the general solution of creating provincial data protection agencies has considerable merit, the political realities of the 1980s seem to make it unlikely that most Canadian provinces will move in this direction in time to have a real impact on two-way services. When a province has no meaningful data protection legislation for the public sector, as in Ontario, one can hardly expect the statutory protection of privacy in two-way services to be the first order of business.

The western provinces of Alberta, Manitoba and Saskatchewan have crown-owned telephone companies that own most of the hardware in the existing cable systems. As required by the CRTC, local cable companies generally own the local headend, the amplifiers and the drops to households. Although such an arrangement has some advantages in terms of integrating technology, government ownership makes obvious the need for regulation— i.e., in order to restrict government access to personal information held in such systems.

In a province like Ontario there is no statutory regulation of a commercial transaction between a subscriber and a company offering two-way services. Similarly, except for the credit reporting field, there are no statutory regulations in Ontario covering retention of personal information involved in such transactions. Policies governing the retention of personal information derived from commercial transactions are largely a matter of corporate policy. The Ontario Consumer Reporting Act of 1973 does provide some model data protection through regulation of private-sector agencies that collect and provide personal information on consumers to credit grantors, employers and other interested third parties.[31]

As discussed in Chapter 2, Quebec is the only province that has passed legislation for data protection in the public sector.[32] Although Law 65 does not extend to such a private-sector activity as the provision of interactive services, the general principles of fair information practices can be applied in order to establish minimum standards for the protection of privacy.

The Ontario government has made little progress in its efforts to implement the 1980 recommendations of the Williams Commission on Freedom of Information and Individual Privacy.[33] While the principles and recommendations of this commission on the need for data protection were designed to apply only to the public sector, they too can be extended to cover the private sector as well. This would at least establish the minimum standards of protection to which the public, including subscribers to interactive services, is entitled. If the Ontario government were to create a data protection agency with responsibility for broad research and the assumption of an advisory role for privacy problems in both the public and private sectors, then the issue of privacy in two-way services could be easily evaluated. However, since the Ontario government has been moving forward so slowly in this important area, it seems unlikely that statutory protections will be in place in time to have an appropriate impact on such an activity.

Given the absence of general legislation for data protection in Ontario, one promising avenue for statutory intervention would be the proposed Telecommunications Act that the Ontario Ministry of Transportation and Communications is developing. One practical argument in favor of this initiative is that Ontario contains almost half of the 50 largest cable systems in the country, including 725,000 Rogers subscribers and 230,000 subscribing to Maclean Hunter systems, as well as more than 40% of all Canadian cable subscriber households.[34] The Ontario initiatives could be similar to our previously suggested amendment of the comparable federal legislation to include provisions on data protection for all two-way services. (These may become necessary if the CRTC or the federal government proved unwilling to regulate non-programming services, which seems unlikely.)

The Ontario Ministry of Transportation and Communications has stated that the province should regulate cable television on the grounds that it is within provincial jurisdiction.[35] It believes that the CRTC has been too restrictive in its attitude toward the development of new cable television services. Regulation of cable also fits into the economic goals of the province. In addition, the Ontario government will be providing information services to the public by means of cable and does not want to be regulated by the CRTC. Yet, given the lack of successful general initiatives for data protection in the province, it would be surprising if the Ministry was willing to take specific steps on its own for the protection of cable privacy. Its primary goal at present is to promote economic opportunities for new cable services by encouraging the federal government to regulate in a more flexible, efficient and responsive manner.[36]

Canadian cable television companies have come to accept being federally regulated and fear the prospect of any sort of additional provincial regulation of cable television services. Generally speaking, they are also strongly interested in deregulation. A few companies in Ontario see a greater chance of that happening if control over certain types of cable activities were in the hands of a provincial government. On the other hand, the major cable television operators with outlets across Canada fear the consequences of two-tier regulation. Smaller cable television companies may be more likely to welcome provincial regulation.

At present, the Canadian provinces are at least making noises about the need for privacy legislation in the private sector, which is an additional stimulus to self-regulation. In January 1984 the Quebec Minister of Justice announced the formation of a task force to recommend legislation to control the use of personal information in private data banks.[37] In May 1984 the Ontario government held a conference on the theme of "Privacy: Initiatives for 1984." Despite the fact that this coincided with the government's introduction of its own weak bill on "Privacy and Access to Information" for the public sector, the conference paid particular attention to the need to regulate the private sector.[38] Various representatives of the private sector, including the Canadian Cable Television Association, reported on their efforts at self-regulation to date. Yet immediately after the public conference, at a private meeting attended by government officials from across Canada, it was agreed that a group of officials from the provinces should study the issues of regulation in both the public and private sectors and report back to a meeting of government ministers within the year.

REGULATION OF THE TELEPHONE INDUSTRY IN CANADA

The North American telephone industry's experience with self-regulation and the protection of confidentiality is directly relevant to the current volume. Because the telephone industry also offers interactive services, it has been forced to confront problems comparable to the issues currently facing the cable television industry. In fact, one defensive explanation cable companies offer to justify the scope of their information-handling activities in two-way services is the assertion that they are acting just like the telephone companies. At the same time, cable and telephony are in direct competition with one another for delivery of the same interactive services to the home. In Canada both types of services are regulated by the CRTC; the telecommunications arm of the CRTC regulates Bell Canada and B.C. Telephone, but not the other provincial telephone companies. Bell Canada, however, is regulated by federal statute as a common carrier, which is not the same as the status of the cable television companies under the Broadcasting Act. It acts "solely as a common carrier, and shall neither control the contents nor influence the meaning or purpose of the message emitted, transmitted or received. . . ."[39] In fact, this status was reconfirmed and reemphasized when the CRTC recently recommended federal legislation 1) to prohibit the Bell group from holding broadcasting or cable television licenses; 2) to require Bell Canada to act solely as a common carrier; and 3) to prohibit it from controlling or influencing the contents of any message it transmits.[40]

Bell Canada is a good example of a major company that handles a considerable amount of personal information and that has taken significant steps to develop appropriate policies for the protection of privacy and confidentiality in its operations. The company has adopted a series of policies and practices designed to highlight the importance of protecting privacy.[41] Its internal handbook for employees begins with a discussion of privacy:

> It's the duty of every employee to respect the customer's privacy and to treat as strictly confidential any personal or business information about the customer that may come to his or her attention. This applies to both oral and written information belonging to the customer, whether it is picked up on either Bell's or the customer's premises. We have a legal as well as moral responsibility to protect the privacy of communications. . . .The content or nature of any telephone call or data transmission—or even the existence of such a message—is not to be made known by Bell employees to any third party.[42]

Although neither the special federal statute that regulates Bell Canada nor the General Regulations for federally regulated telephone companies explicitly refer to protecting the confidentiality of personal information, the company has developed a basic policy, identified as "Bell Canada's practices on the confidentiality of records" in a company manual. Bell does not consider confidential the name, address and telephone number associated with the listed number of an individual, since subscribers can choose whether or not to have their phone numbers listed in a local telephone directory. The rest of the personal information collected by Bell is considered private and is held on a need-to-know basis within the company. Personal data are not sold; such data include long-distance telephone records, credit records, billing records and unlisted telephone numbers.

The company will only release confidential personal information in compliance with a court order, such as a subpoena or a search warrant, obtained by the police or other proper authority: "Bell's policy is to tell the customer that his records have been seized by the police—except in the case where the court order specifically states that we are not to tell the person."[43] It has been suggested that Bell Canada's policies on the latter point are such that some law enforcers regard the company as uncooperative. Others allege that law enforcers obtain regular, informal access to long-distance toll records from local company offices. There is, of course, no public record on how often third parties obtain informal or unauthorized access to Bell's records on individuals. Nor is there any evidence available as to the extent to which Bell's general policies on confidentiality are enforced and obeyed in daily practice.

One relevant practice concerning confidential personal information has to do with Bell Canada's record retention policies for long-distance calls. Formerly, billing information had been kept for three months, but because of a switch to a new computer system, Bell Canada now retains details of individual long-distance calls for six months. After this period records are destroyed through reuse of the computer tapes. Thereafter Bell Canada only has a record of the total long-distance usage in dollars but not the details of individual calls. While it is a matter of opinion whether six months is an appropriate retention period, the protection of privacy position would favor a return to the former practice of a three-month retention period.

Another Bell Canada practice directly relevant to the data transmission activities of companies offering two-way services has to do with wiretapping. Official company policy is as follows: "An essential feature of all our communication services is the undisputed right of the user to privacy, and the company will continue to do its utmost to preserve this right. However, when presented with a wiretap court order, the company will cooperate with law enforcement agencies to the extent contemplated by the law."[44] In response to a court order, Bell Canada will provide certain information but "will not install or assist in the physical establishment of any wire tap." The company also has policies to be followed in the event that an employee discovers a wiretap in place.

Wiretapping in Canada is regulated by the federal Protection of Privacy Act of 1974, which promotes wiretapping more than it does privacy. It seems likely that this statute could also cover the tapping, bugging and disclosure of intercepted private communications made over coaxial cable.[45]

In its two-way Vista experiments, using the telephone and a television set, Bell Canada was able to apply its standard practices and policies on confidentiality to the new interactive services. Bell was directly responsible for the operation of Vista and remained the only company in this venture dealing directly with users, until the teleshopping experiment began in the fall of

1982. In the latter case, an individual signed a consent form allowing his or her name to be forwarded to the supplier of the goods, and Bell simply acted as a common carrier.

The most relevant practice developed by Bell Canada in connection with its Vista field trials was the requirement of contracts between Bell Canada and the subscriber/participant and Bell Canada and the information provider. The participants were private individuals cooperating, at no cost to themselves, in the Vista field trials. Although the five-page contract between Bell Canada and the participant typically imposed more obligations on the individual than on the company, there is a provision in Section 9 on confidentiality, discussed in Chapter 4.

Bell Canada also entered into contractual agreements with the information providers in the Vista field trials. The standard contract provides in Section 14 that all contact with the subscribers shall be made by Bell Canada or persons authorized in writing by Bell Canada. The general provision on confidentiality is in Section 19 and states:

> Each party hereto respectively agrees that all information provided to it by the other party which is identified as confidential shall be deemed the property of the first party and that, (except as otherwise provided herein), such information shall be: (i) held and used in confidence; (ii) disclosed only to those employees or agents who have a need for it under, or by reason of this agreement; and (iii) used only for the purpose of performing any function, conducting any study or taking any action under, or by reason, or in connection with this agreement.

These types of standard contractual agreements can furnish a model for other companies in the self-regulation of their relations with subscribers and information providers in the course of offering interactive services.

The Telephone Industry's Responsibilities to the Public

With respect to the issues treated in this section, 33% of respondents in the London Privacy Survey (see Chapter 2) did not trust the telephone company to use personal information it collects only for the purpose of providing services to customers. Eight percent of respondents thought that the telephone company collects much more personal information than it needs, 32% thought that the telephone company collected somewhat more personal information than it needs, and 58% thought that the telephone company collected only the personal information that it needs.[46]

The results of the London Privacy Survey suggest that the public image of the telephone company with respect to the protection of privacy and confidentiality is not as good as it could be. Bell Canada's own analysis of survey data concluded that "telephone invasions of privacy rank high as a perceived possibility in both societies–slightly higher in Ontario than in the U.S."[47] The general public requires further assurances in this regard; the inclusion of formal, specific policies on confidentiality in the General Regulations for federally regulated telephone companies would be a step in the right direction.

Telephone companies should engage in some internal and external con-sciousness-raising with respect to the protection of personal privacy, especially as they begin to be associated with two-way services. Although the companies may argue that they already have standard policies in place for the protection of confidentiality, these offer inadequate assurances to the general public, given the risks to personal privacy inherent in the large-scale data processing activities related to two-way services.

It is not difficult to pinpoint the appropriate contents for telephone privacy regulations. The Louis Harris 1979 privacy poll in the U.S. showed a very high positive consumer response to such practices as telling people why information is needed, how the information will be used, and obtaining the consent of the individual before releasing identifiable personal information. In the London Privacy Survey 91% of respondents stated that cable com-panies should inform subscribers what information they were collecting and how it will be used, and 96% believed that they should have to furnish written permission for use of any such identifiable information by cable firms.[48] When asked whether government intervention was necessary to pre-vent abuses of personal information, or whether the cable companies should be left alone to develop their own privacy codes, 72% favored government intervention while 17% favored self-regulation.

In essence, privacy regulations should apply a code of fair information practices to telephony.[49] These elements can be reviewed in detail in any of the existing North American and European data protection laws, and in the OECD's *Guidelines for the Protection of Privacy and Transborder Flows of Personal Data* (1981). Fair information practices involve minimizing intru-siveness into personal lives, maximizing the use of informed consent, holding the telephone company ultimately responsible for maintaining the confiden-tiality of all personal information flowing through its computer systems, and releasing only aggregated (non-identifiable) personal information to third parties under normal circumstances.

SELF–REGULATION BY COMPANIES OFFERING INTERACTIVE SERVICES

Despite all the technical, regulatory and economic problems that they are facing, it is clear that companies offering interactive services should provide within their operations a framework for the protection of personal privacy, especially as they introduce two-way services. Although cable companies may argue that they already have standard policies in place for the protection of confidentiality, these are completely inadequate to deal with the risks to personal privacy inherent in the large-scale information-processing activities related to two-way services.

All companies can avoid or at least minimize external regulation by initiating measures for data protection in their various information-handling practices. It is to the advantage of the regulators and the regulated to encourage as much self-regulation as possible in order to handle current and prospective problems. It will also help to discourage the creation of an additional regulatory bureaucracy for data protection in the private sector.

The argument in favor of self-regulation in the cable industry coincides with recommendations made in Canada by John Lawrence, vice-chairman of the CRTC, industry consultants such as Frank Spiller, and, most recently, by the CRTC itself.[50] The argument for self-regulation in the U.S. advanced in 1981 by Collingwood Associates seems compelling:

> The companies in the interactive home media business are capable of, and may wish to, establish standards for protecting consumer privacy for their corporate entities. They can also work together to develop industry-wide standards in this area. We recommend that these standards be developed formally, that they be written policies and procedures for protecting privacy. We further recommend they be part of the contracts between consumers and service providers and that consumers be notified of changes in the services as they occur.[51]

In engaging in self-regulation with respect to the protection of privacy, companies offering interactive services will be following the lead of other private-sector groups in Canada, the United States and Western Europe. Such Canadian insurance companies as Aetna Casualty Company of Canada, London Life and The Excelsior Life Insurance Company have adopted general privacy codes.[52] In 1982 the Bank of Montreal published its code on privacy and confidentiality, which was discussed in Chapter 4. Cable television and videotex companies can also follow the admirable lead of Warner Amex Communications, the New York State Cable Television Association, the U.S. Videotex Industry Association and the Canadian Cable Television Association in developing privacy codes. Finally, the U.S. National Cable Television Association has recently initiated mechanisms to develop an industry-wide code on privacy, as recommended by such observers as Alan F. Westin.[53]

For at least a decade IBM has been among the private-sector leaders in developing good internal policies for the protection of privacy and confidentiality. In December 1981 IBM Europe published its "Guidelines for an Internal Program for Protection of Personal Data," which can serve as a model for self-regulation by companies offering two-way services. IBM applies these guidelines to its worldwide operations. The IBM introduction makes two important points: "Although the concern with the potential misuse of personal data may sometimes seem to be excessive, the need for privacy protection and data security is legitimate. Each organization that collects, stores, processes, and disseminates personal data should assume the responsibility to define its personal data protection principles and its data security organization." Several of the basic principles of data protection enunciated by IBM have direct relevance to interactive services: "The purpose of any application or file that handles personal data should be clearly defined and shown to be in support of valid Company business needs....Only the personal data that is needed for the defined purposes of an application or file may be collected. . . .Personal data should be used, communicated, and retained only to the extent necessary for the defined purposes of the application or file."[54] The remainder of the IBM document contains very explicit directions on the organization and implementation of a data protection program.

One advantage of self-regulation is that, after the basic framework of a privacy code has been put in place, it can continue to evolve in response to emerging problems. In an interview with CBC Television early in 1982, Gustave Hauser, then chairman of Warner Amex, noted that "we are still an evolving business and I think most regulation is premature. We are in effect regulating ourselves as we see the problems and if they exist." Thus a key element of Warner Amex practice is that the company "shall continuously review and update its Code of Privacy to keep current with technological changes and new applications."

One major Canadian MSO is developing a subscriber privacy policy, which has gone through several drafts.[55] If put into effect, it could have an impact on other Canadian cable companies. Internal company response to the draft code for its Canadian and U.S. operations has varied from a positive reaction to a desire not to make the privacy policy overly restrictive; indeed, a number of senior employees are aware that information collected on individuals may become a valuable resource.

It seems logical that the effort to adopt company subscriber privacy policies for cable should start with the leading Canadian MSOs, since they are the ones introducing or most likely to be introducing two-way services. They are also most likely to have had experience with the privacy issue in the U.S. A relevant precedent for several major Canadian cable companies who also operate systems in the U.S. has been their acceptance of the privacy and confidentiality provisions in U.S. local ordinances and contracts as part of the franchising competition in municipalities.

The most significant and commendable Canadian step toward self-regulation took place in June 1984 when the general membership of the

Canadian Cable Television Association adopted a cable industry subscriber privacy policy for its 380 member companies serving 4.8 million subscribers. The new policy, which appears in full in an appendix to this volume, is essentially the same as eight of the eleven points in the Warner Amex code. The CCTA code does not address the issues of releasing aggregated information, preparing subscriber mailing lists, and complying with applicable laws and industry codes, which are points 4, 8 and 9 in the Warner Amex code. It would be most desirable for such organizations as the Canadian Videotex Industry Association and the Videotex Information Service Providers Association of Canada to undertake similar initiatives at self-regulation.

Self-regulation obviously presents a number of problems in implementation; not the least of these is persuading individual companies offering interactive services that they should be concerned with the problem of privacy protection. It is one thing to argue that companies should do good, but another to persuade them successfully to implement appropriate policies and procedures. Even if specific appropriate policies are recommended by an industry association, member companies choose individually whether or not to implement these. The example of one or two companies that have committed themselves to privacy protection is also not necessarily a stimulus to the rest of the industry. In the U.S., for example, Warner Amex remains the only major cable operator that has developed and adopted its own privacy code.

The Canadian cable television industry is made up of a few large companies and a great many small ones. Since the largest multi-system operators are much more professionalized than the smaller operators and individual companies, self-regulation may not work in practice for the latter. If many small local cable companies became involved in offering two-way services, which seems unlikely in the near future, the possibilities for misuse of personal information might increase, making the necessity of government intervention even stronger. There may be additional problems in devising an appropriate role in data protection for the active provincial cable television associations in Ontario, Quebec and Alberta, where resistance to more government regulation is strong. There is also the difficulty of devising a suitable scheme to ensure the protection of personal privacy and confidentiality on the part of information and service providers as well as by the cable television company itself.

Although it is always difficult to predict the real costs of data protection for any information system, there is no reason to believe that the costs companies will incur in protecting privacy will be excessive or even significant. A crucial argument in favor of low costs is that appropriate protections can still be incorporated in the design stage of software systems and hardware configurations. Rogers Cablesystems Inc., the leading Canadian company, has already incorporated a number of appropriate measures in its American two-way cable systems. Postponing protective measures for privacy will only add to a cable company's costs at a later stage of two-way cable development. (The West German and Swedish experiences with data protection further suggest that good data protection promotes efficient flows of personal information during data processing activities.) The costs of protecting privacy may not be minor, especially if a company actually wants to sell identifiable data about subscribers, but the costs of not protecting privacy can also be high, if potential subscribers to two-way services develop resistance to the intrusive aspects of permitting such systems to be installed in their households.

The issues for personal privacy raised by two-way services are in many ways not much different from the standard challenges posed by all the new technological innovations of the last 20, and indeed, last several hundred, years. One need only reflect on the problems for personal privacy posed by the introduction of the telegraph and the telephone in the second half of the nineteenth century.[56] Unfortunately, even in these cases, if privacy problems were recognized, little was done about them. History shows that privacy has too frequently either been ignored or sacrificed with equanimity to such competing values as progress, efficiency and commercial gain. The private sector may regard this history of *laissez-faire* as a compelling model for the present; however, the extent of the threat to personal privacy posed by automated personal information systems today is so great that there must be a move toward self-regulation in the private sector, reinforced by as much government regulation as proves necessary.

NOTES

1. Department of Communications, *Towards a New National Broadcasting Policy* (Ottawa: Dept. of Communications, 1983). Bill C-20 is discussed in *Cable Communications Magazine*, L (March 1984), pp. 9–11.

2. The Canadian Radio-television Telecommunications Commission Act, S.C. 1974-75-76, C. 49. Excellent details on how the CRTC operates can be found in C. C. Johnston, *The Canadian Radio-television and Telecommunications Commission. A Study of Administrative Procedure in the CRTC* (Ottawa: Law Reform Commission of Canada, 1980). For a critique of the CRTC's general regulatory role, see Stan Feldman and Hudson Janisch, "Pay-TV: Jurisdictional and Regulatory Issues," in R. Brian Woodrow and Kenneth B. Woodside, eds., *The Introduction of Pay-TV in Canada. Issues and Implications* (Montreal: Institute for Research on Public Policy, 1982), pp. 102–113.

3. Broadcasting Act, R.S.C. B-11. The act defines a cable company as a "broadcast receiving undertaking."

4. Broadcasting Act, ss. 15, 16(1)(b)(9). See, generally, Lorne P. Salzman, "Home Videotex Services: Some Legal Issues," *The Canadian Journal of Information Science*, VI (1981), pp. 17–18.

5. *Cable Television Regulations,* SOR/75-665, s. 5.

6. *The London Free Press,* October 21, 1982, p. A2.

7. Canadian Radio-television and Telecommunications Commission, *Decision. Decision CRTC 81-920 and Decision CRTC 82-921* (Ottawa: Canadian Radio-television and Telecommunications Commission, December 30, 1981). (Hereafter cited as CRTC, *Decision.*)

8. 38 Newfoundland and P.E.I. R. 224; 108 APR 224. The denial of the motion for leave to appeal is in 46 NR 623. See Jonathan Chevreau, "Court Decision Seen Harmful to Domestic Cable Sector," *The Globe and Mail,* October 21, 1982, p. B7.

9. *The Globe and Mail,* November 6, 1982, p. B2.

10. Canadian Cable Television Association, *The 1980's Challenge: New Consumer Services Through Cable Television.* Special Report. Plenary IV, CCTA Annual Convention, Vancouver, May 1980 (Ottawa: Canadian Cable Television Association, 1980), p. 2. (Hereafter cited as CCTA, *The 1980's Challenge*); Canadian Radio-television and Telecommunications Commission, "Public Hearings on Non-programming Services," Toronto, March 10–12, 1981, pp. 256, 328. (Hereafter cited as CRTC, *Hearings.*)

11. CRTC, *Hearings,* Vancouver, April 28–30, 1981, pp. 315, 317.

12. CRTC, *Hearings,* Toronto, March 10–12, 1981, pp. 216, 217–218, 237, 255; see also CRTC, *Hearings,* Vancouver, April 28–30, 1981, p. 412.

13. CCTA, *The 1980's Challenge,* p. 3; Charles Dalfen, *An Industry in Transition. Regulatory Aspects of the New Technology,* Royal Commission on Newspapers Research Reports, April 6, 1981, pp. 95, 106, 108, 110, 123–124; see also Francis Spiller Associates, *New Broadcasting and Communications Services (A Perspective)* (Nepean, Ontario: Francis Spiller Associates, September 1980), pp. 47, 63–66, 76.

14. Canadian Radio-television and Telecommunications Commission, *Notice. A Review of Certain Cable Television Programming Issues* (Ottawa: Canadian Radio-television and Telecommunications Commission, March 26, 1979), pp. 5–6.

15. CRTC, *Hearings,* Vancouver, April 28–30, 1981, p. 327; Home Office, *Report into Cable Expansion and Broadcasting Policy* (1982), p. 7.

16. The text of this public announcement can be found in Dalfen, *Industry in Transition,* pp. 83–84.

17. Canadian Radio-television and Telecommunications Commission, *Public Announcement,* "Non-programming Services by Cable Television Licensees," Ottawa, March 26, 1979, pp. 2-3. (Hereafter cited as CRTC, *Public Announcement.*)

18. Canadian Radio-television and Telecommunications Commission, *Decision. Decision CRTC 79-276* (Ottawa: Canadian Radio-television and Telecommunications Commission, March 26, 1979).

19. See the comments by Ted Rogers and Ed Jarmain, then Chairman of CTRI, in CRTC, *Hearings,* Toronto, March 10–12, 1981, p. 236; and Vancouver, April 28–30, 1981, p. 295.

20. CRTC, *Introductory Statement Relating to Decisions 81-919 to 81-922, Applications for the Cable Distribution of Non-Programming Services on an Experimental Basis.* (Ottawa: Canadian Radio-television and Telecommunications Commission, December 30, 1981.)

21. CRTC, *Decision, CRTC 81-919, 81-920, 81-922.*

22. *Ibid.,* pp. 4, 6, 7.

23. CRTC, *Decision 82-473* (Ottawa: Canadian Radio-television and Telecommunications Commission, May 31, 1982).

24. CRTC, *Notice. Ownership of Equipment for the Delivery of Pay Television Services by Licensed Cable Television Undertakings* (Ottawa: Canadian Radio-television and Telecommunications Commission, April 22, 1983).

25. CRTC, *Public Notice: CRTC 1983-245. Cable Television Service Tiering and Universal Pay Television Service* (Ottawa: Canadian Radio-television and Telecommunications Commission, October 26, 1983), pp. 19–20.

26. *House of Commons Debates* 124, No. 370, June 28, 1982, Column 18854; S.C. 1980-81-82, C. 111, Schedule II. See the discussion in Chapter 2.

27. An Act to enact the Access to Information Act and the Privacy Act, S.C. 1980-81-82, c. 111.

28. This proposal is discussed in the *Report of the Privacy Commissioner on the Use of the Social Insurance Number* (Ottawa: Privacy Commissioner and Department of Justice, 1981), pp. 211–217. This number is the equivalent of the Social Security Number in the U.S. The enactment of criminal law is primarily a federal matter in Canada, whereas in the U.S. most criminal laws are enacted by the individual states.

29. *Ibid.*, pp. 215–217. In testimony before the Subcommittee on Computer Crime of the House of Commons Standing Committee on Justice and Legal Affairs in Ottawa on May 3, 1983, I argued for the desirability of criminal sanctions against unauthorized disclosure of, or unauthorized access to, automated personal information in both the public and private sectors. See House of Commons, *Minutes of Proceedings and Evidence of the Sub-Committee on Computer Crime of the Standing Committee on Justice and Legal Affairs,* Issue No. 5 (May 3, 1983), pp. 18–36 and appendix 5A, pp. 1–25.

30. Lawrence Surtees, "DOC starting major review," *The Globe and Mail,* Oct. 6, 1983, p. B5.

31. R.S.O. 1980, c. 89. There is a useful report of this law in Ontario, *Public Government for Private People. The Report of the Commission on Freedom of Information and Individual Privacy* (Toronto, 1980), pp. 658–661. See also Dale Gibson, "Regulating the Personal Reporting Industry," in Dale Gibson, ed., *Aspects of Privacy Law* (Toronto: Butterworths, 1980), pp. 111–140.

32. An Act respecting access to documents held by public bodies and the protection of personal information, S.Q. 1982, c. 30.

33. *Public Government for Private People,* Chapters 32–35.

34. *Cable Communications Magazine,* XLIX (November 1983), pp. 48–49; and Canadian Radio-television and Telecommunications Commission, *Facts Digest* (January 1982), p. 6. (Hereafter cited as CRTC, *Facts Digest.*)

35. Newfoundland has passed a bill to assert its jurisdiction over non-broadcasting services on cable and other modes of telecommunications. (An Act to amend the Public Utilities Act, S.N. 1982, c. 24, s. 1.) Minister of Communications, Norman Doyle, specifically mentioned such services as tele-shopping, security services, information retrieval and opinion-polling.

36. At the annual meeting of the Ontario Cable Television Association in Toronto in October 1982, Ontario Minister of Transportation and Communications, James Snow, reportedly said that the new telecommunications legislation being drafted by his department does not contain a section pertaining to the cable industry, as it once did, simply because the province now has no reason to believe that it will acquire jurisdiction over cable through negotiation with the federal Minister of Communications. (Eric Bender, "Abolition of CRTC Urged by B. C. Minister," *The London Free Press,* October 21, 1982, p. A2); see also *The London Free Press,* October 6, 1983.

37. *The Globe and Mail,* January 17, 1984, p. 5.

38. See Ontario, Provincial Secretariat for Resources Development, *Discussion Paper on Privacy: Initiatives for 1984* (Toronto, 1984), Part III; and the report on the Toronto conference in *Privacy Times,* IV, No. 11 (June 6, 1984), pp. 6-9.

39. Bell Canada Special Act, S.C. 1967-8, c. 48, s. 6. On the relationship between the CRTC and the telephone company, see Lewis Auerbach, "Privacy and Canadian Telecommunications Regulation," *Telecommunications Policy* (March 1983), pp. 37-39. The complexities of the regulation of Canadian telecommunications are explored in Robert J. Buchan, C. Christopher Johnston, T. Gregory Kane, Barry Lesser, Richard J. Schultz and W. T. Stanbury, *Telecommunications Regulation and the Constitution* (Montreal: The Institute for Research on Public Policy, 1982).

40. David Stewart-Patterson, "CRTC Feels Bell Reorganization May 'Impair' Power to Regulate," *The Globe and Mail,* April 19, 1983, p. B11.

41. This volume suggests that these should be formally incorporated in the General Regulations of the CRTC for all federally regulated telephone companies. See David H. Flaherty, "Confidentiality of Subscriber Information. Comments on the CRTC's Discussion Paper: 'Review of the General Regulations of the Federally-Regulated Telephone Companies' (1983)," memorandum submitted to the CRTC, November 1, 1983. These regulations have remained essentially unchanged since 1953.

42. Bell Canada, *Our Code of Business Ethics,* pp. 3-4.

43. Presentation by Jeff Campbell, Bell Canada, to the National Secretaries' Association and the Business and Professional Women's Association, Montreal, March 24, 1981, p. 3. Other special practices by which Bell Canada releases personal information under emergency circumstances are not discussed here.

44. Bell Canada, General Circular 101.42, Wire Taps, June 1974.

45. The 1974 act is discussed in a two-part series by Jeff Sallot, *The Globe and Mail,* July 2, 1984, p. 1; and *The Globe and Mail,* July 3, 1984, p. 8; David Deutscher, "The Protection of Privacy Act: Whose Privacy is it Protecting?" in Gibson, ed., *Aspects of Privacy Law,* pp. 141-162; and Eugene G. Ewaschuk, *Criminal Pleadings and Practice in Canada* (Aurora, Ontario: Canada Law Book Ltd., 1983), Chapter 4.

46. Neil J. Vidmar, "Privacy and Two-way Cable Television: A Study of Canadian Public Opinion" (Downsview, Ontario: Ontario Ministry of Transportation and Communications, May 1983), table 5.

47. Bell Canada, "Public Attitudes Toward the New Micro-Technologies" (May 1982), p. 28. After reviewing issues of individual privacy and telephone

companies, Lewis Auerbach concluded that "in general, Canada does not have adequate laws or regulations to protect consumers from misuses of information about them." (Auerbach, "Privacy and Canadian Telecommunications Regulation," *Telecommunications Policy* [March 1983], p. 39.)

48. Louis Harris & Associates, Inc. and Alan F. Westin, *The Dimensions of Privacy. A National Opinion Research Survey of Attitudes Toward Privacy.* (Stevens Point, WI: Sentry Insurance: 1979), pp. 88–90; Vidmar, "Privacy and Two-Way Cable Television," pp. 44–45, table 14.

49. I offered specific proposals for General Regulations on privacy and confidentiality for federally regulated telephone companies in Canada in Flaherty, "Confidentiality of Subscriber Information," a memorandum to the CRTC, dated November 1, 1983.

50. See a report of a speech by Lawrence in *Computing Canada,* October 14, 1982, p. 42, and Spiller, *New Broadcasting and Communications Services,* pp. 73–74, 76–77; CRTC, *Public Notice, CRTC 1983-245,* p. 20.

51. Deanna Collingwood Nash and John B. Smith, *Interactive Home Media and Privacy.* Prepared for the Office of Policy Planning, U.S. Federal Trade Commission (Washington, DC: Collingwood Associates, Inc., January 1981), p. 16.

52. The right to privacy guidelines of the Canadian Life Insurance Association are printed in Ontario, *Report of the Commission of Inquiry into the Confidentiality of Health Information* (3 vols., Toronto, 1980), II, pp. 232–234.

53. Alan F. Westin, "Home Information Systems: The Privacy Debate," *Datamation,* XXVIII, No. 7 (July 1982), pp. 112–113.

54. IBM Europe, *Guidelines for an Internal Programme for Protection of Personal Data* (obtainable from local IBM offices). See also J. K. Williams, "European Data Protection—a Business Viewpoint, *Transnational Data Report,* V, No. 3 (1982), pp. 156–160.

55. See the discussion in Daphne Lavers, "Subscriber Privacy in Two-Way Systems," *Cable Communications Magazine,* L (March 1984), p. 20.

56. See David J. Seipp, *The Right to Privacy in American History* (Cambridge, MA: Harvard University Program on Information Resources Policy, Publication P-78-3, 1978).

8

Summary and Conclusions

OVERVIEW OF THE KEY PRIVACY ISSUES IN TWO-WAY SERVICES

New York Attorney General Robert Abrams has argued that interactive cable television is going to generate "the single largest repository of personal data and information in the history of the world." If this allegation is correct, and there are compelling reasons to think that it is, then two-way services pose considerable challenges to individual privacy and the confidentiality of personal information. Companies offering interactive services must be encouraged to develop and implement provisions and guidelines on confidentiality and privacy that will limit the collection, storage and use of personal information to legitimate business purposes in such a manner that subscriber interests are protected at all times. Contrary to the customary practices of most private concerns, companies will have to be persuaded that there are appropriate limits on the uses of personal information that comes into their possession through the operation and use of two-way systems.

A fundamental principle for companies to observe is that of informed consent on the part of subscribers, who should be made aware of what information will be collected from them and exactly what will be done with it. They should have the right to know that the company will not use data on individual subscribers for any purposes beyond those set forth in an explicit contract with subscribers. An appropriate code of fair information practices should further establish the right of a subscriber to correct any erroneous information. Fortunately, leaders in the development of two-way cable services—such as Warner Amex, which offers QUBE in Columbus and other cities—have given assurances that individual records are used only for billing purposes and are destroyed after nine months.[1] As two-way services continue to develop, other cable companies should be urged to initiate similar policies.

Another issue which should command the attention of companies offering two-way services is the risk that a dishonest or corrupt employee will use or release personal information in an unauthorized manner. At present some

143

major multi-system operators require that all their employees sign a form concerning the confidentiality of subscriber lists. This practice should be extended to cover the much larger range of personal information that will become available to company headend computers when two-way systems are fully developed. The risk of unauthorized use or disclosure exists in any information system and can have irreversible consequences for individuals. This is not an imagined or inflated concern fantasized by privacy advocates but a practice that has already surfaced in other communications and information industries. The California Department of Consumer Affairs, for example, is currently investigating what some believe to be a growing number of firms involved in selling confidential customer long-distance telephone records. It has been alleged that a group of employees within the Pacific Telephone Company is selling customer phone records to banks, collection and repossession companies, and detective agencies.[2] Security Pacific National Bank acknowledged that it had fired five employees at one branch for purchasing telephone records from the phone company. In order to reduce the risks of unauthorized release of information about subscribers, all companies will have to establish guidelines on data confidentiality and will have to initiate appropriate security measures.

A further major issue concerns the need to design software in such a way as to minimize the storage in company computers of identifiable personal information; at the same time, this would render less possible the creation of profiles of individuals by integrating personal information derived from various sources. Minimizing the retention of identifiable personal information will contribute greatly to the ultimate protection of subscriber privacy. To the maximum extent, identifiable individual information should only be stored when it is essential for billing purposes and subsequently destroyed or placed in inactive files as relevant law or practice requires. Software for such services as public opinion-polling should be designed in such a manner that it is impossible for anyone to learn the views of a particular subscriber. (As noted in Chapter 4, straightforward software design of this type requires no additional expenditures by a cable company, so long as the planning is done in the design stage.) In addition, separate modules should be used for tele-education and opinion-polling, and the software for information retrieval systems should not record the actual information that subscribers have requested, except to the minimum extent necessary for billing procedures. For example, it might be possible to record simply the actual page number that a subscriber retrieved from a particular information base rather than storing the descriptive content of what was retrieved. If retrieval is charged for only on the basis of computer time used, it would also prevent storage of data about information actually retrieved.

Provincial and state laws normally regulate the amount of time for which information on consumer transactions has to be stored. In the U.S. laws on record-keeping are sometimes designed to allow the state to monitor complaints against a company and also to measure the gross revenues of the cable company, since the franchising fee is usually a percentage of gross revenues. State statutes of limitation concerning the time period within which an individual can bring a lawsuit against a firm further determine the number of years business enterprises must keep records of individual transactions.[3] This is not always the case in Canada. Ontario commercial law, for example, tends not to specify the record retention requirements for personal information.

Along with the concern for minimizing storage of identifiable personal data is the need to design software in a way which will reduce the possibilities for record linkages and the compilation of profiles of subscribers using a variety of different two-way services. In theory a detailed user profile can be constructed from information collected in a fully operational two-way cable system. Gardner and White have pointed out "the growing attractiveness of private sector matching operations" in their report to the New York Consumer Protection Board.[4] For a large company like Rogers Cablesystems, which has local franchises across Canada, it will also be important that data sharing about subscribers be kept to an absolute minimum. From the point of view of confidentiality, all data processing activities, for billing and other purposes, would preferably take place within the confines of the individual local franchise, with only minimal amounts of personal data to be transferred to a central agency. Cableshare Ltd. of London, Ontario formerly handled billing for all local Rogers cable TV operations, but on an outlet-by-outlet basis with no integration of files. The economic incentives for a multi-system operator to centralize customer billing services in one location, as in the case of Cableshare (which also services non-Rogers cable companies), do not extend to actual integration of data from separate local systems. However, the potential payoffs from selling national, provincial or metropolitan lists of certain types of subscribers could become very significant financially, which is why subscribers must be given valid assurances that cable companies do not sell or release identifiable data about them without explicit permission. Companies offering two-way services need to design their data processing centers in a manner that encourages the processing of subscriber information with the maximum attention paid to confidentiality and security.

It is also necessary to design appropriate protections for the physical security of personal information handled in two-way systems.[5] Many privacy problems can be dealt with through additional technology, such as the use of computers to monitor computers and the encryption of sensitive personal information moving between the host computer and home terminals. James Martin, an expert in this field, has made several relevant and timely points about the important issue of security: "the technology for data bank security is now understood. However, most of today's data banks are grossly insecure—most of them are not protected at all." Recent press stories about computer "hackers" reinforce this basic point. In Martin's opinion, electronic protection of data will eventually become a standard part of computer technology. He concludes that the legal framework for the protection of privacy must "be one that lends itself to the maximum automation. The computer must keep check on the computers. Only in this way can the ultimate system be workable."[6] Such practices would be of considerable assistance in furnishing subscribers with legitimate expectations of confidentiality that are also enforceable against cable companies and/or information or service providers.

Yet the evidence continues to accumulate that appropriate security measures are not fully utilized. For example, of the world's eight largest banks "only four do any encryption at strategic locations. . . ."[7] A senior security official of the U.S. Department of Health and Human Services told a meeting of the American Society of Access Professionals in Washington, DC on November 18, 1982 how difficult it is to persuade personnel to follow established security practices, including the use of encryption in a few instances where it is already available.

Security is particularly important in the headend computer operations of companies with two-way systems. It can include such practices as a card-lock system to keep premises physically secure, audit trails, double passwords for access to polling and security functions, and triple passwords for record-keeping functions, which can be changed every day.[8]

Two-way systems also involve the transmission of a significant amount of personal information over cable or telephone lines. Currently, cable has about the same security as a telephone line. However, if the need is perceived to exist, customer data passing upstream through a cable can be encrypted. Telecable Videotron normally does encryption on its communication lines, using standard protocols, because the experience of senior systems designers has indicated the importance of such a practice. A company such as Videotron also has a variety of internal reasons to be careful about security. For one thing, security plays a vital part in the company's overall plans to ensure accuracy in its information systems. For another, it also has to impose security to restrict customer access to services that have not been ordered. Since cable companies scramble their signals going downstream in order to protect against theft of the product being delivered to the home, transmission of personal data upstream might also be scrambled in order to protect its confidentiality. Technical devices as small as a silicon chip costing $250 are available, at least in the United States, that can achieve the U.S. federal government Data Encryption Standard.

The sheer volume of personal information transmitted in all two-way systems will furnish some protection for privacy, confidentiality and security, although the capacity to store data should not be underestimated. The American National Security Agency, for example, has developed the capacity "to monitor continuously nearly every international telephone conversation or message to or from anyone in the United States." All telephone calls carried by microwave transmission in or into Canada are probably monitored in a similar fashion by the ultra-secret Communications Security Establishment of the federal government in Ottawa.[9] It is therefore especially important that cable and telephone companies make a conscious decision to retain in identifiable form only such personal information on subscribers as is necessary for legitimate business purposes.

A related security issue, which will require continued study and monitoring, concerns the possibility of a third party intercepting cable TV signals from a neighboring home. Because the data signals of a particular house are on the cable system, at least in the immediate vicinity of the home, they would automatically resonate into the cables of individuals living nearby. With an interactive system, in theory a neighbor knowing the right techniques could pick up and record the upstream messages of his neighbor. He could listen to this data traffic in a way that is not possible with the telephone system. Collingwood Associates regarded this as an "improbable activity" because of the difficulty of designing a device to do the tapping. Moreover, some technical protections could be adopted to prevent the practice.[10]

Yet another issue affecting the privacy and confidentiality of personal information in two-way systems is the extent to which a company simply functions as a common carrier (the term is used here in a practical, not a legal, sense) for information or service providers, as is the usual case for telephone companies. The roles and responsibilities of the information providers and the common carriers or system operators overlap and need to be treated together. It would be inappropriate for a company offering two-way services to argue that it loses control over personal information once it has been passed on to a service or information provider, such as a retailer. As the American privacy expert Willis Ware pointed out at a Washington conference in May 1982, the new privacy problems do not involve the regulation of large data banks of personal information, as in the past, but in controlling such systems as two-way cable, where information is not stored in large data bases and is not solely used for record-keeping purposes, but is often in transit to third parties.[11] In my opinion, the cable or telephone company should be held legally responsible for ensuring the confidentiality and security of all personal information moving through its systems, even if it decides to extend this liability by contracts with other information or service providers which lease capacity on the two-way system.

A further problem for privacy and confidentiality is regulating third-party access to personal information derived from two-way cable or telephone services. This is one of the thorniest issues facing companies, and one for which external regulation by legislatures or other authorities is probably necessary. Restricting unrestrained government access to all types of personal information in private hands is one critical offshoot of this issue. The 1978

Right to Financial Privacy Act, whatever its other limitations, established in the U.S. procedures whereby governments could only have access to individual banking records after the individuals concerned were notified in advance. The example of an attorney attempting to secure access to QUBE viewing records in Columbus, Ohio (discussed in Chapter 4) indicates that such concern is not purely hypothetical.

In general, personal information held in the private sector does not enjoy any kind of privileged status at present with respect to third-party access. Persons or organizations with an alleged need to know will seek access to any existing data bases that may appear suitable for a particular purpose. In its privacy code Warner Amex states that it "will refuse requests to make any individual subscriber information available to government agencies in the absence of legal compulsion, i.e., court order, subpoena. If requests for such information are made, Warner Amex will promptly notify the subscriber prior to responding if permitted to do so by law." Even this admirable statement of intentions has a number of loopholes in it, which will have to be addressed by laws or regulations developed with the assistance of regulatory authorities in both the United States and Canada.

This volume recommends the following overall scenario for coping with real and hypothetical concerns of subscribers about privacy in two-way services. A primary goal is to encourage Canadian and American cable companies through their trade associations to self-regulate by developing and adopting codes of privacy similar to the Warner Amex code in the United States. Given the currently slow pace of introduction of two-way cable services, the current efforts at self-regulation of the Canadian Cable Television Association and various state cable associations are very important steps in the right direction. The 1984 Canadian code can be presented to the CRTC as evidence of a responsible approach by the industry to privacy problems. If self-regulation does not produce concrete results, various federal, state and provincial legislative and regulatory agencies should take appropriate steps to intervene for the protection of privacy in all two-way systems.

After reviewing a draft of this study early in 1983, the Executive Committee of the Canadian Cable Television Association directed its staff to explore the development and implementation of policies for protecting the privacy of cable subscribers. Its board of directors subsequently accepted the principle of developing a privacy code with the assistance of the association's Financial Control and Reporting Committee, which has cross-Canada representation of senior officers responsible for the financial management of cable companies, including the major multi-system operators. This process resulted in the Association's adoption of a "Cable Subscriber Privacy Policy" in June 1984, which should now be adopted by individual cable companies.

Self-regulation has innumerable advantages yet it cannot solve all of the potential privacy problems of two-way services. The issue of regulating third-party access to stored subscriber records is a problematic one, which will probably require legislation. Whatever policies and procedures the various companies have in place, law enforcers and government agencies, for example, will seek access by formal and informal means; the legitimacy of, and procedures for, such access will have to be established.

In a general way the respondents to the London Privacy Survey reflected concerns about the inadequacies of self-regulation and about problems of third-party access. After the survey discussed attractions of two-way cable services, along with their accompanying challenges to privacy, a question was asked about willingness to let the cable companies self-regulate to handle these problems, as this current volume recommends. Eighty-eight percent of respondents wanted government regulation of information collection and storage in two-way systems. When the issue was then posed in terms of cable company regulation through self-developed privacy codes versus government regulation, only 17% were willing to leave the matter to the cable companies, whereas 72% still wanted government regulation. Thus the sampled population in London displayed very little sympathy with the customary private-sector view that it is already overregulated. In fact, the 210 households in the sample trusted the public sector even more than the private sector when it comes to the collection and proper use of personal information, with 51% of respondents expressing trust in federal and provincial governments versus 38% trusting businesses and companies. Finally, 98% of respondents favored strict regulations to minimize the possibility of an employee of a cable company providing information to outsiders or to prevent someone from the outside penetrating security barriers and stealing personal information.[12]

For a full understanding of why two-way cable systems pose more risks to privacy than practices on the part of other communications and information industries, it is imperative that the reader remember one final point mentioned several times in this volume. Although it is true that fully operational interactive systems will be capable of collecting more information on individuals than ever before possible, it is the status of the industry providing two-way services that puts in potential jeopardy the confidentiality of personal data; cable companies, for a number of reasons already discussed, are in a financially vulnerable position where the economic benefits of selling individual data might provide overwhelming temptations to breach subscriber privacy. It is for this reason that self-regulation, both on a company-by-company and industry-wide basis, coupled with legislative regulatory action, is urgently necessary. Going hand in hand with such regulatory measures is the need for subscriber recourse to the courts in the form of penalties imposed on those companies that have compromised a subscriber's trust by the misuse or release of personal information gathered in the course of operating two-way systems.

CONCLUSIONS AND RECOMMENDATIONS

1. Survey results in Canada and the United States demonstrate that individuals are very concerned about protecting their personal privacy in the face of the widespread introduction of new information and communications technology.

2. Two-way cable television and telephone services pose a substantial threat to the personal privacy of subscribers by making possible the accumulation, storage and dissemination of large amounts of identifiable information about individuals and households.

3. Whether the threats to personal privacy are real, prospective or primarily hypothetical, public fears should be allayed and continued sensationalism avoided by the introduction of responsible and adequate measures for data protection in two-way services.

4. Cable television companies and their trade associations should immediately develop and implement policies for protecting the privacy of their subscribers through a code of fair information practices, as has been done in the United States by Warner Amex and the New York State Cable Television Association, among others, and in Canada by the Canadian Cable Television Association.

5. Privacy codes should be made part of contractual agreements with individual subscribers, so that they might have a right of action against the cable or telephone company, if a breach of confidence or an invasion of privacy is alleged to have occurred.

6. Companies offering two-way services should refuse to sell, give or release any identifiable data on subscribers to third parties without either the express consent of the subscriber, or in response to a court order or a subpoena.

7. Companies offering two-way services should be held legally responsible by subscriber contracts for ensuring the security and confidentiality of identifiable subscriber data flowing through their cable and telephone systems to information and service providers.

8. The Canadian Radio-television and Telecommunications Commission should incorporate a code of fair information practices as an integral part of the conditions governing the licensing of non-programming services offered by cable television companies. The adequacy of the Canadian Cable Television Association's 1984 privacy code can be reviewed at CRTC hearings and incorporated at least in outline form in the conditions for licensing non-programming services.

9. If the cable television industry and individual cable companies in North America fail to self-regulate for purposes of data protection, and/or regulatory agencies such as the CRTC fail to pursue their expressed concern for privacy and security by developing relevant standards, then the federal

governments in the United States and Canada and/or state and provincial legislatures will have to enact special data protection statutes or include new provisions in existing or revised acts, comparable to the several state cable privacy laws already in place in the United States.*

Legislative intervention may also be necessary if joint cable industry/ cable company initiatives fail to provide subscribers with methods of pursuing claims for invasion of privacy, including the availability of criminal sanctions for unauthorized disclosure of personal information and protection against third-party access to personal data on subscribers held by cable companies.

---

*As this book was going to press, President Reagan signed into law the Cable Communications Policy Act of 1984 after it had passed through both houses of Congress. The privacy provisions in this act are reprinted in Appendix B at the back of this volume.

NOTES

1. Deanna Collingwood Nash and John B. Smith, *Interactive Home Media and Privacy.* Prepared for the Office of Policy Planning, U.S. Federal Trade Commission (Washington, DC: Collingwood Associates, Inc., January 1981), p. 52.

2. See *Privacy Times* II, No. 5 (August 4, 1982), pp. 2–3; Andrew Pollack, "Computer Ethics: Questions Arise on Misuse in Business," *The New York Times,* December 25, 1983, pp. 1, 26; *The Globe and Mail,* January 2, 1984, p. 7.

3. Sidney L. Gardner and Robin White, *New Technology and the Right to Privacy: State Responses to Federal Inaction. A Report to the New York State Consumer Protection Board.* (Unpublished draft, August 1982), p. 37 note.

4. *Ibid.,* p. 71. Matching refers to the linkage of diverse bodies of personal data on individuals for a new purpose. Governments sometimes match records from separate departments, and it is possible for different units of one or several private companies to do the same.

5. I have discussed the implications of computer-based crime for personal privacy in Canada in House of Commons, *Minutes of Proceedings and Evidence of the Sub-committee on Computer Crime,* Issue No. 5, May 1983 (Ottawa: Canadian Government Publishing Centre, 1983), pp. 18–36 and appendix 1, pp. 1–25.

6. James Martin, *The Wired City* (Englewood Cliffs, NJ: Prentice-Hall, Inc. 1978), pp. 259, 261, 262–263.

7. J. Michael Nye, "Satellite Communications and Vulnerability," *Computerworld*, XVI, No. 18 (May 3, 1982), In-Depth, p. 11.

8. Nash and Smith, *Interactive Home Media and Privacy,* p. 51; for a technical description of the QUBE security system in Columbus, see pp. 45–46.

9. James Bamford, *The Puzzle Palace. A Report on America's Most Secret Agency* (Boston: Houghton Mifflin, 1982), pp. 174, 261–263, 297 and 305; compare also, pp. 331–332 for similar activities in the U.K. For the Communications Security Establishment, see "Secret listening agency expands its operations," *The Globe and Mail,* November 12, 1983, p. 3.

10. Nash and Smith, *Interactive Home Media and Privacy,* pp. 49–50. On the problem of cable pirates, see *The New York Times,* August 24, 1983, p. B2.

11. Ware predicted increasing attention to the problem of protecting privacy in interactive cable systems. (*Privacy Journal,* VIII, No. 8 [June, 1982], p. 2.)

12. Neil J. Vidmar, "Privacy and Two-Way Cable Television: A Study of Canadian Public Opinion," (Downsview, Ontario: Ontario Ministry of Transportation and Communications, May 1983), pp. 20, 23, 45, 46, 49.

Appendix A:
Selected Privacy Codes

1. WARNER AMEX CABLE COMMUNICATIONS*
Code of Privacy (1981)

1. Warner Amex shall explain to its subscribers the information gathering functions of the cable communications services being provided.

2. Warner Amex shall maintain adequate safeguards to ensure the physical security and confidentiality of any subscriber information.

3. Warner Amex subscriber agreements shall include the following:

   a. Individual subscriber viewing or responses may be recognized only where necessary to permit billing or to render a subscriber service. Any such information will be kept strictly confidential unless publication is an inherent part of the service (e.g., announcing a game show prize-winner).

   b. No other individualized information concerning viewing or responses will be developed unless the subscriber has been advised in advance and given adequate opportunity not to participate.

4. Warner Amex may develop bulk (non-individual) data concerning subscriber services for use in developing new services or improving existing services. Warner Amex will not make such bulk data available to third

---

*Warner Amex Cable Communications, 1981. Reprinted with permission of Warner Amex Cable Communications.

parties—whether affiliated or nonaffiliated with Warner Amex—without first ensuring that the identity of individuals is not ascertainable from the data provided.

5. Warner Amex will refuse requests to make any individual subscriber information available to government agencies in the absence of legal compulsion, i.e., court order, subpoena. If requests for such information are made, Warner Amex will promptly notify the subscriber prior to responding if permitted to do so by law.

6. Subscribers may examine and copy any information developed by Warner Amex pertaining to them at Warner Amex premises upon reasonable notice and during regular business hours. Copying costs shall be borne by the subscriber. Warner Amex shall correct such records upon a reasonable showing by the subscriber that information contained therein is inaccurate.

7. Any individual subscriber information will be retained for only as long as is reasonably necessary, e.g., to verify billings.

8. Subscriber mailing lists shall not be made available to third parties—whether affiliated or nonaffiliated with Warner Amex—without first providing subscribers with the opportunity to have their names removed from such lists.

9. Warner Amex shall comply with applicable Federal, State and local laws respecting subscriber privacy and shall adhere to applicable industry codes of conduct which promote or enhance subscriber privacy.

10. Third parties who participate in providing services to Warner Amex subscribers shall be required to adhere to the Company's Code of Privacy and all Warner Amex arrangements regarding such services shall specifically incorporate this Code of Privacy by reference.

11. Warner Amex shall continuously review and update its Code of Privacy to keep current with technological changes and new applications.

2. THE CANADIAN CABLE TELEVISION ASSOCIATION CABLE SUBSCRIBER PRIVACY POLICY*

In order to properly respond to the subscribers' current and future needs, the cable operators must record certain specific information regarding the subscribers' residence and service preferences. The cable industry is aware of its responsibility to maintain subscriber information on a confidential basis.

The cable industry undertakes to continue to maintain subscriber information in a manner consistent with the goal of affording maximum protection from the invasion of privacy to all cable service subscribers.

Franchise commitments and regulations may vary in different areas of Canada. Notwithstanding, the cable industry subscriber privacy policy shall contain as a minimum the following principles:

1) *Subscriber Education*

   Cable companies shall explain to subscribers to a particular service the information gathering functions of the service being provided.

2) *System Design & Privacy*

   a) The cable licensee shall take all reasonable steps necessary to ensure the physical security of the cable system.

   b) Data collected shall remain within the individual cable system except for authorized inter office corporate transactions.

   c) Access to data collected from each subscriber's residence shall be restricted to those employees directly concerned with the operation of the service involved.

   d) Data collected from each subscriber residence will be retained only as long as is necessary (e.g. for billing purposes) and will then be destroyed.

   e) Information regarding subscriber viewing and/or responses will be recorded only where necessary to permit billing or to provide adequate service to the subscriber.

---

*The Canadian Cable Television Association, June 13, 1984. Reprinted with permission.

    f)   No other individualized data concerning viewing habits or responses shall be recorded unless the subscriber has been informed in advance.

3) *Agreements with Third Parties*

Adherence to the Cable Subscriber Privacy Policy shall be required of all third parties that may participate in providing services to the cable companies' subscribers.

4) *Subscriber Access to and Verification of Information*

    a)   Subscribers shall be allowed reasonable access to verify the accuracy of any information pertaining to them which is developed by the company. Upon reasonable notice, subscribers may examine and copy such personal information at the company's premises during regular business hours. The cost of copying such information shall be borne by the subscriber.

    b)   Upon a reasonable showing by the subscriber that information pertaining to him/her in the company's files is inaccurate, the company shall undertake to correct such information without delay.

5) *Legal Compliance*

    a)   Information pertaining to individual subscribers will be made available to government agencies only under court order or other legal compulsion.

    b)   Where permitted by law, subscribers shall be made aware of such legal requests for information.

6) *Privacy Policy Review*

The cable industry shall review this policy once a year at a minimum to ensure that current legal and technological developments are addressed where necessary.

3. VIDEOTEX INDUSTRY ASSOCIATION
MODEL PRIVACY GUIDELINES
FOR VIDEOTEX SYSTEMS*

Preface

In the next few years, millions of Americans will be using videotex systems to obtain information, send messages, and do shopping and banking from home. The companies that run videotex systems and those that provide services through videotex operators will have to keep records on many of these uses. The Videotex Industry Association has adopted guidelines to suggest how those records should be collected and used.

These guidelines are not binding, and some companies may alter some of the specifics. However, the guidelines do represent a commitment by the videotex industry to a basic principle—that subscribers should be told what information about them is being collected and how it will be used.

There have been no privacy abuses in the videotex industry. This voluntary effort by the industry should help keep that record pure and should help inspire consumer confidence in this new technology.

John Woolley
Chairman Fair Practices Committee

Richard Neustadt
Vice Chairman Fair Practices Committee

Introduction

As with many consumer services, two-way electronic information systems create records on subscriber usage. Information must be recorded to process subscribers' requests, maintain technical operations, prevent improper use, manage billings, conduct market research, and improve the service. These guidelines explain how these records will be collected and used and how subscriber privacy will be protected.

Coverage

These guidelines apply to all subscriber records, whether stored on paper or in electronic form, that are collected through use of a videotex system and are in the system operator's control.

---

*Videotex Industry Association, June 1983. Reprinted with permission.

Notice

On the initiative of the system operator, each subscriber will be provided with a written or electronic copy of these guidelines.

Bulk Information

"Bulk information" means aggregate records that do not identify individual subscribers. For example, information about types of subscribers, such as those in a geographic area or demographic category, is bulk information. The system operator may use bulk information for its own purposes and may disclose such information to others.

Individual Information

"Individual information" means records that identify individual subscribers. The system operator may collect and use individual information for the following reasons: (1) to provide service in response to a subscriber's request; (2) to maintain technical operations; (3) to prevent illegal or unauthorized use of the videotex system; (4) to manage and operate billing and accounting systems; and (5) to conduct market research in order to compile bulk information. Individual information will not be used or disclosed for any other purpose without obtaining written or electronic consent from the subscriber and giving him or her the opportunity to refuse, except for disclosure in response to compulsory process as set forth in the section on Government Access.

Any consent sought under this section will specify the types of information covered and the purpose of the use or disclosure. The system operator will not exclude any subscriber from any videotex service for declining to provide such consent. A subscriber may revoke consent by written or electronic notice to the system operator.

Government Access

The system operator will not disclose individual information to government agencies except in response to compulsory process (e.g., subpoena or court order) or with the subscriber's consent. Unless a court orders otherwise, the system operator will promptly notify the subscriber if a court or government agency seeks access to individual information in conjunction with an investigation of the individual. Unless a court orders otherwise, the system operator will withhold disclosure of subscriber records demanded under compulsory process for a reasonable period after notice is sent to the subscriber, to give the subscriber time to contest such disclosure. In addition, the system operator may, in its discretion, contest any demands for disclosure that it feels would jeopardize confidence in the privacy of the system and may co-operate with the subscriber in opposing such disclosure.

Security

The system operator will make all reasonable efforts to safeguard individual information against unauthorized access.

Subscriber Access

Subscribers may obtain copies of any individual information developed by the system operator pertaining to them, upon reasonable notice and during regular business hours. Copying and other reasonable costs shall be borne by the subscriber.

Correction of Errors

The system operator will promptly correct any errors or omissions in its records that are brought to its attention by subscribers. The system operator may request appropriate documentation to verify any such errors or omissions.

Application to Third Parties

Banks, retailers and other organizations use videotex systems to provide services to subscribers, and they maintain their own records of such transactions. The system operator will give these service providers a copy of these guidelines and encourage them to adhere to the guidelines.

Future Revisions

The system operator may alter these guidelines to conform to federal and state laws, to reflect changes in technology, or to improve its service. Each subscriber will be notified of any such change.

Retention of Information

Individual information will be retained only as long as it is needed for the purposes for which it was collected.

Appendix B:
Cable Communications Policy
Act of 1984, Section 631

PART IV—MISCELLANEOUS PROVISIONS

PROTECTION OF SUBSCRIBER PRIVACY

SEC. 631. (a) (1) At the time of entering into an agreement to provide any cable service or other service to a subscriber and at least once a year thereafter, a cable operator shall provide notice in the form of a separate, written statement to such subscriber which clearly and conspicuously informs the subscriber of—

(A) the nature of personally identifiable information collected or to be collected with respect to the subscriber and the nature of the use of such information;

(B) the nature, frequency, and purpose of any disclosure which may be made of such information, including an identification of the types of persons to whom the disclosure may be made;

(C) the period during which such information will be maintained by the cable operator;

(D) the times and place at which the subscriber may have access to such information in accordance with subsection (d); and

(E) the limitations provided by this section with respect to the collection and disclosure of information by a cable operator and the right of the subscriber under subsections (f) and (h) to enforce such limitations.

In the case of subscribers who have entered into such an agreement before the effective date of this section, such notice shall be provided within 180 days of such date and at least once a year thereafter.

(2) For purposes of this section, the term 'personally identifiable information' does not include any record of aggregate data which does not identify particular persons.

(b) (1) Except as provided in paragraph (2), a cable operator shall not use the cable system to collect personally identifiable information concerning any subscriber without the prior written or electronic consent of the subscriber concerned.

(2) A cable operator may use the cable system to collect such information in order to—

(A) obtain information necessary to render a cable service or other service provided by the cable operator to the subscriber; or

(B) detect unauthorized reception of cable communications.

(c) (1) Except as provided in paragraph (2), a cable operator shall not disclose personally identifiable information concerning any subscriber without the prior written or electronic consent of the subscriber concerned.

(2) A cable operator may disclose such information if the disclosure is—

(A) necessary to render, or conduct a legitimate business activity related to a cable service or other service provided by the cable operator to the subscriber;

(B) subject to subsection (h), made pursuant to a court order authorizing such disclosure, if the subscriber is notified of such order by the person to whom the order is directed; or

(C) a disclosure of the names and addresses of subscribers to any cable service or other service, if—

(i) the cable operator has provided the subscriber the opportunity to prohibit or limit such disclosure, and

(ii) the disclosure does not reveal, directly or indirectly, the—

(I) extent of any viewing or other use by the subscriber of a cable service or other service provided by the cable operator, or

(II) the nature of any transaction made by the subscriber over the cable system of the cable operator.

(d) A cable subscriber shall be provided access to all personally identifiable information regarding that subscriber which is collected and maintained by a cable operator. Such information shall be made available to the subscriber at reasonable times and at a convenient place designated by such cable operator. A cable subscriber shall be provided reasonable opportunity to correct any error in such information.

(e) A cable operator shall destroy personally identifiable information if the information is no longer necessary for the purpose for which it was collected and there are no pending requests or orders for access to such information under subsection (d) or pursuant to a court order.

(f) (1) Any person aggrieved by any act of a cable operator in violation of this section may bring a civil action in a United States district court.

(2) The court may award—

(A) actual damages but not less than liquidated damages computed at the rate of $100 a day for each day of violation or $1,000, whichever is higher;

(B) punitive damages; and

(C) reasonable attorneys' fees and other litigation costs reasonably incurred.

(3) The remedy provided by this section shall be in addition to any other lawful remedy available to a cable subscriber.

(g) Nothing in this title shall be construed to prohibit any State or any franchising authority from enacting or enforcing laws consistent with this section for the protection of subscriber privacy.

(h) A governmental entity may obtain personally identifiable information concerning a cable subscriber pursuant to a court order only if, in the court proceeding relevant to such court order—

(1) such entity offers clear and convincing evidence that the subject of the information is reasonably suspected of engaging in criminal activity and that the information sought would be material evidence in the case; and

(2) the subject of the information is afforded the opportunity to appear and contest such entity's claim.

Selected References

This volume is based upon interviews and the miscellany of sources cited in the notes at the end of each chapter. *The New York Times* and *The Globe and Mail*'s "Report on Business" devote considerable attention to the developments treated above. Two Washington-based newsletters are also very valuable, *Privacy Journal*, which is edited by Robert Ellis Smith, and *Privacy Times*, edited by Evan Hendricks.

For valuable introductions to both the new information technology and its societal implications, see: Tom Forester, ed., *The Microelectronics Revolution. The Complete Guide to the New Technology and Its Impact on Society* (Cambridge, MA, 1981); James Martin, *The Wired Society* (Englewood Cliffs, NJ: Prentice-Hall, 1978); Simon Nora and Alain Minc, *The Computerization of Society. A Report to the President of France* (Cambridge, MA: The Massachusetts Institute of Technology Press, 1980); *Technology and Privacy. The Report of the Privacy Protection Study Commission. Appendix 5* (Washington, DC, July 1977); Lance J. Hoffman, ed., *Computers and Privacy in the Next Decade* (New York: Academic Press, 1980); U.S. Congress, Office of Technology Assessment, *Computer-Based National Information Systems. Technology and Public Policy Issues* (Washington, DC: U.S. Government Printing Office, 1981).

For a general introduction to the enormous amount of literature on privacy, see David H. Flaherty, Edward H. Hanis and S. Paula Mitchell, eds. *Privacy and Access to Government Data for Research. An International Bibliography* (London, U.K.: Mansell, 1979), pp. 1-26, 100-127; and Flaherty, ed., *Privacy and Data Protection: An International Bibliography* (London, U.K.: Mansell, 1984; Knowledge Industry Publications, Inc., 1984).

The most relevant literature on privacy and interactive services includes Alan F. Westin, "Home Information Systems: The Privacy Debate," *Datamation*, XXVIII, No. 7 (July 1982), p. 104; John Wicklein, *Electronic Nightmare: The New Communications and Freedom* (New York: The Viking Press,

1979); Deanna Collingwood Nash and John B. Smith, *Interactive Home Media and Privacy*. Prepared for the Office of Policy Planning, U.S. Federal Trade Commission (Washington, DC: Collingwood Associates, Inc., January 1981); Sidney L. Gardner and Robin White, *New Technology and the Right to Privacy: State Responses to Federal Inaction. A Report to the New York State Consumer Protection Board*. (Unpublished draft, August 1982.) A revised version will be published in 1984 by the New York State Consumer Protection Board; Fred W. Weingarten, "Information Technology and Privacy Trends in Products and Services," in *Invited Papers on Privacy: Law, Ethics, and Technology*. Presented at the National Symposium on Personal Privacy and Information Technology, (Washington, DC: American Bar Association, 1982), pp. 15–26; Stephen Console, "Cable Television Privacy Act: Protecting Privacy Interests from Emerging Cable TV Technology," *Federal Communications Law Journal*, XXXV (1983), pp. 71–94; David Burnham, *The Rise of the Computer State* (New York: Random House, 1983).

An article by Neil Vidmar and David H. Flaherty ("Concern for Personal Privacy in an Electronic Age") presenting the results of the London Privacy Survey (which is discussed in the text) is forthcoming in 1985 in the *Journal of Communications*.

Index

167

ABOUT THE AUTHOR

David H. Flaherty, professor of history and law at the University of Western Ontario, London, Canada, has had a long involvement with the study of personal privacy. His professional interest began in 1964 when, as a graduate student in American history at Columbia University, he worked as a research assistant to Alan F. Westin, author of *Privacy and Freedom* (Atheneum, 1967). Flaherty subsequently undertook the first intensive investigation of the concept of privacy in an historical context, which was published as *Privacy in Colonial New England* (University Press of Virginia, 1972). In 1974 he began a study funded by the Ford Foundation of the privacy problems involved in using personal information collected by government statistical agencies for research and statistical purposes. Research in North America and three European countries led to the publication of *Privacy and Government Data Banks. An International Perspective* (Mansell, 1979).

In 1978 Flaherty completed a study for the Ontario government of the implications for privacy and confidentiality of creating an electronic funds transfer system in Canada. In 1979 he prepared a report on research and statistical uses of personal data for the Ontario Commission on Freedom of Information and Individual Privacy. In 1981 he conducted a study for the Federal Privacy Commissioner on the origins and development of social insurance numbers in Canada.

Flaherty is currently in the process of completing a long-term research project on how privacy and data protection laws for the public sector are working in practice in six countries. This project is funded by the Ford Foundation and the Social Sciences and Humanities Research Council of Canada. In 1983 he finished a study for the Ontario government entitled, *Protecting Privacy: Data Protection in Two-Way Cable Television Services,* which included a survey of attitudes toward privacy protection. This volume represents a revised and expanded version of that study.

In December 1982 Flaherty testified before a U.S. Senate Subcommittee in hearings on computer matching; in May 1983 he testified on the privacy implications of computer crime before a Subcommittee of the Canadian House of Commons; and in June 1983 he participated in the first oversight hearings on the U.S. Privacy Act of 1974 before a Subcommittee of the U.S. House of Representatives.

Flaherty organized and chaired an international conference on "Privacy and Data Protection: Nineteen Eighty-Four and After," which was held at the Bellagio Study and Conference Center on Lake Como, Italy, in April 1984, with the support of the Rockefeller and Ford Foundations.

Flaherty has taught at Princeton University (1965-1968) and the University of Virginia (1968-1972). From 1971 to 1972 he was a Fellow in Law and History at the Harvard Law School, and during 1978-1979 a Visiting Fellow at Magdalen College, Oxford. In 1972 he joined the faculty of the University of Western Ontario. In 1984 he became the first director of Western's Centre for American Studies, a research institute designed to promote understanding of the United States.

At present Flaherty is a member of an Advisory Panel, Office of Technology Assessment, U.S. Congress, for a study of Federal Government Information Technology and its implications for civil liberties. He is also a contractor for the Office of Technology Assessment for a study of "Data Protection and Privacy—Comparative Policies."